GW00359446

THE
INTERESTING
BITS

The History You Might Have Missed

JUSTIN POLLARD

MARKS &
SPENCER

Marks and Spencer p.l.c
PO Box 3339
Chester CH99 9QS

s h o p o n l i n e

www.marksandspencer.com

Copyright © 2007 by Justin Pollard

First published in Great Britain in 2007
by John Murray (Publishers)
An Hachette Livre UK company

The right of Justin Pollard to be identified as the Author of the
Work has been asserted by him in accordance with the Copyright,
Designs and Patents Act 1988.

All rights reserved. Apart from any use permitted under UK
copyright law no part of this publication may be reproduced, stored
in a retrieval system, or transmitted, in any form or by any means
without the prior written permission of the publisher, nor be
otherwise circulated in any form of binding or cover other than that
in which it is published and without a similar condition being
imposed on the subsequent purchaser.

ISBN 978-0-7195-2413-4

Printed and bound in Spain

Disclaimer
The views expressed in this book are those of the author but they
are general views only and readers are urged to consult a relevant
and qualified specialist for individual advice in particular situations.
Marks and Spencer p.l.c hereby exclude all liability to the extent
permitted by law for any errors or omissions in this book and for
any loss, damage or expense (whether direct or indirect) suffered
by a third party relying on any information contained in this book.

CONTENTS

Introduction   vii

1 Oops!

Which king rode off a cliff?   2
Who went into exile after breaking wind?   3
Where does the Bible recommend adultery?   3
Why couldn't you read Marie Curie's lab notes until the
   1990s?   4
Which general was accidentally shot by his own troops?   5

2 Surprise, Surprise!

Who was Miss Canary Islands 1936?   8
What was the star attraction at the Bronx Zoo in 1906?   8
Which monument was bought as a birthday present?   10
What was Oliver Cromwell's name?   11
Who gave all three of his sons the same name?   12

3 Men of the Cloth

Whom did Edward Gibbon accuse of piracy, murder, rape,
   sodomy and incest?   14
Which famous monk married a nun?   15
Who cremated Jesus Christ?   16
Who made 200 monks jump?   18
How old was the youngest pope?   19

4 Heads

What did Walter Raleigh's wife keep in her handbag?   22
Who hung the world's most famous painting in his
    bathroom?   23
How did one man's ear start a war?   24
Which general gave his name to facial hair?   25
Which English king breathed fire then expired?   26

5 What's in a Name?

Who was Gordon Bennett?   30
Who is the Bob in 'Bob's your uncle'?   31
Who was the first nosy parker?   31
Who formed the first lynch mob?   33

6 Animal Magic

What was the Battle of the Herrings?   36
Who were the victims of the War of the Currents?   37
What was unusual about Thomas Hobson's stable?   39
How did Dracula get his name?   40
Who fought the Dog Tax War?   41

7 Bedhopping

How did Charles the Mad stop his wife having an affair?   44
Who preferred adultery to a pint of beer?   45
Who said 'cock-a-doodle-doo' to a bishop?   45
Who is the only member of the royal family to be sued for
    adultery?   46
Did George I go to bed with an elephant?   47

8 Ouch!

What was the 'extraordinary question'?   50
Which king died from a splinter?   50
How do you play mediaeval football?   51
What did the Empress Irene, Ivan the Terrible,
    Süleyman the Magnificent and Constantine the
    Great have in common?   53

9 Magic

Why did Dick Whittington need a magical cat?   56
Who was rescued by the Queen of Elfland?   57

10 Unsound Minds

What do French lawyers and rats have in common?   60
Who liked kissing her dead husband's feet?   61
What did Alexandra of Bavaria believe she had
    swallowed?   63

11 Bang!

How long did the gunfight at the OK Corral last?   66
How could Annie Oakley have prevented the
    First World War?   66
Who ruined the Parthenon?   67
Which English king exploded?   68
What nineteenth-century game involved smashing
    snail shells?   70

12 Unlucky

What was the Ball of the Burning Men?   72
Who has the record for the shortest reign?   73
Who gave his name to nationalistic zealotry?   73
Why might it be dangerous to drink weak beer?   74
What made William the Miserable so unhappy?   75

13 How Did That Happen?

How did Erik Bloodaxe get his name?   78
Why did Joan of Arc fight the English?   78
Why did Lady Godiva get her kit off?   80
How did Calamity Jane get her name?   81

14 Who?

Why were there 212 fatalities at the first boy scout camp?   84
Which world leader drew the poster for Teddy's
    Perspiration Powder?   85
Who was Dirty Dick?   86
Which twentieth-century British king was murdered?   87

INTRODUCTION

History is *not* more or less bunk, despite what Henry Ford said. In fact he probably only made the comment in the hope that no one would listen to future historians when they said things like, 'Did you know that Adolf Hitler kept a photograph of Henry Ford in his study?'

There is one problem with history, however – there is an awful lot of it. Everyone and everywhere seems to be full of it. This presents a writer with a problem: how do we understand what's going on? How do we make sense of all this . . . stuff? Traditionally there have been two answers:

1. Write a huge number of impenetrable books, each about a tiny bit of history, with titles like *The Custard Cream as Social Metaphor – 1967 to 1971*.
2. Write sweeping narratives in which everything is neatly arranged into lists of places, peoples and dates. A suitable title might be *A Complete History of Civilisation from the Earliest Times, in Thirty-Six Volumes*.

Neither of these approaches is without its problems, and the biggest of these is that there's a real danger that they make the whole thing extremely boring. You end up with too many books that you know you'll never read about subjects you'd like to know a bit about, but frankly not quite *that* much. Or you find yourself with a few huge tomes full of lists of rulers, lists of battles, lists of important pieces of Hebridean highways legislation – and endless lists of dates.

This is why children don't listen in history lessons at school and who can blame them? Where's the fun? Where's the intrigue? Where are the interesting stories of the mad, bad, stupid, wonderful, odd and improbable things that happened to our ancestors? The past is as daft as the present and the people of the past were as daft as us. That's what actually links us.

History is not simply the extension of the present back into the past; it is a very strange and very different country. Nor does history have a grand direction, although many history books imply that it does. History wanders around, often drunk, frequently bumping into things and usually eschewing anything that might look like progress for another sustained period in full reverse.

So rather than try to produce another volume on custard creams or a big *History of Everything*, which won't actually include everything but rather consist of another series of lists that are impossible to remember, *The Interesting Bits* is more of a selection box – a didactic mixture of historical delicacies, stories, events, facts (and a few salacious rumours) that will go no way whatsoever towards helping the reader to pass his or her GCSE History exam. They have no greater meaning, no direction and no overarching theme beyond being, I hope, worthy of note, possibly even memorable and reminding us that the past was no less peculiar than the present. If it must have a purpose, then I suppose it might help in pub quizzes – maybe.

1

Oops!

'There's been an accident,' they said,
'Your servant's cut in half; he's dead!'
'Indeed!' said Mr Jones, 'and please,
Send me the half that's got my keys.'

Harry Graham, *Ruthless Rhymes for
Heartless Homes* (1899)

Which king rode off a cliff?

Alexander III's rule over Scotland was marred by personal tragedy. By 1283 the king had lost his first wife and outlived all of his children. According to the Chronicle of Lanercost, he was not too bothered by loneliness, however, as *'he used never to forbear on account of season nor storm, nor for perils of flood or rocky cliffs, but would visit none too creditably nuns or matrons, virgins or widows as the fancy seized him, sometimes in disguise.'*

This was great fun but it overlooked the fact that he did need an heir. So it was that on 14 October 1285 he married the French heiress, Yolande de Dreux. All looked to be going well and, as he was only forty-four, there still appeared to be time to produce a successor. The following year all that changed. Once again according to the Chronicle of Lanercost, around 19 March 1286, Alexander finished eating a large dinner in Edinburgh and, despite the gathering gloom and the pleas of his nobles, decided to visit his new bride who was a short distance away in Kinghorn. Having crossed the Queensferry,

> he arrived at the burgh of Inverkeithing, in profound darkness, accompanied only by three esquires. The manager of his saltpans, a married man of that town, recognising him by his voice, called out: 'My lord, what are you doing here in such a storm and such darkness? Often have I tried to persuade you that your nocturnal rambles will bring you no good. Stay with us, and we will provide you with decent fare and all that you want till morning light.' 'No need for that,' said the other with a laugh, 'but provide me with a couple of bondmen, to go afoot as guides to the way.'

This was a mistake. The party continued but just two miles down the road, now in complete darkness, they lost their way and Alexander, in his eagerness to reach the nuptial bed, rode straight off a cliff. The bodies of horse and rider were recovered the next morning. Without a surviving heir, Scotland had no king for the next six years.

Who went into exile after breaking wind?

The story of Oxford's embarrassment comes from diarist John Aubrey's *Brief Lives*, a collection of short biographies written towards the end of the seventeenth century. According to Aubrey, Edward de Vere, 17th Earl of Oxford, was bowing particularly low to Queen Elizabeth I one day when he accidentally (and loudly) broke wind. So embarrassed was de Vere that he went into voluntary exile for seven years. Eventually he returned to court and once again found himself in the presence of the Queen. He bowed carefully (and perhaps a little timorously) this time. The intense silence was only broken by Elizabeth commenting, 'My Lord, I had forgot the fart.'

Supporters of the Earl of Oxford, particularly those who believe that he may be the true hand behind the works of Shakespeare, often consider this story a calumny but it was certainly in circulation by the early years of the seventeenth century where it is referenced in the contemporary poem 'The Parliament Fart', which dates from around 1610. Whilst Aubrey's style is gossipy and occasionally a shade saucy, he was usually a meticulous biographer. And anyway, as he put it himself, *'How these curiosities would be quite forgott, did not such idle fellowes as I am putt them down.'*

Where does the Bible recommend adultery?

The book making this rather surprising suggestion is the 1631 edition of the Holy Bible published by the printers Lucas and Barker. Their version, now a rare collector's item, omits the word 'not' from Exodus 20: 14, leaving us with the commandment: *'Thou*

Shalt Commit Adultery.' Thanks to this omission their version is now known as the 'Wicked' Bible, and Lucas and Barker received a hefty fine from King Charles I.

And Lucas and Barker were not the only ones that Charles had his eye on. The 'Fool's Bible' brought its printer a £3,000 fine for reading: '*The fool hath said in his heart, there is a God*' in Psalm 14: 1 instead of '*The fool hath said in his heart, there is not a God.*' The 'Unrighteous Bible' of 1653 used the words, '*Know ye not that the unrighteous shall inherit the kingdom of God*' in I Corinthians 6: 9, again omitting the all-important word 'not'.

In the 'Ears to Ears' Bible of 1807, the line in Matthew 13: 43, '*Who hath ears to hear*', reads '*Who hath ears to ears,*' whilst the 'Standing Fishes' Bible of the previous year replaces Ezekiel 47: 10, '*that the fishers shall stand*', with '*that the fishes shall stand*', conjuring an interesting image.

More modern misprints have some of the cynicism of the age. In a 1966 first edition of the Jerusalem Bible, Psalm 122: 6 reads, '*Pay for peace*' instead of 'Pray', whilst a 1970 first edition of the King James II New Testament has John 1: 5 reading, '*And the light shines in the darkness, and the darkness overcomes it*', instead of '*And the light shines in the darkness, and the darkness does not overcome it.*'

Why couldn't you read Marie Curie's lab notes until the 1990s?

Marie Curie is the only woman ever to win two Nobel prizes, the first person ever to win two, and one of only two people to have won Nobels in different fields (the other being Linus Pauling for Chemistry and Peace).

Her two citations for the prizes give a good clue as to why her lab notes have remained inaccessible. Her 1903 Physics prize, awarded with her husband Pierre Curie and Henri Becquerel, was 'in recognition of the extraordinary services they have rendered by their joint researches on the radiation phenomena discovered by Professor Henri Becquerel', whilst her 1911 Chemistry prize was 'in recognition of her services to the advancement of chemistry by the discovery of the elements radium and polonium, by the isolation of radium and the study of the nature and compounds of this remarkable element'.

When one of Marie's daughters and her granddaughter donated Marie's diaries, journals and workbooks to the Bibliothèque Nationale in Paris in the mid-1990s, it was, perhaps not surprisingly, discovered that they were all still highly radioactive. It took two years to decontaminate the paper before the bequest could be accessioned.

At the outbreak of the First World War, Marie cashed in her Nobel gold medals to help the war effort. She died of leukaemia in 1934, almost certainly caused by her massive exposure to radiation.

Which general was accidentally shot by his own troops?

Thomas 'Stonewall' Jackson was one of the most successful and daring Confederate commanders in the US Civil War. He also had a lifelong belief that one of his arms was longer than the other, which it wasn't.

In his last battle, at Chancellorsville in 1863, the Confederate Army of North Virginia won a major victory over the much larger Union Army of the Potomac, following a brilliant outflanking manoeuvre by Jackson. Unfortunately, whilst returning to camp on 2 May Jackson and his staff were waylaid by one of their own regiments (from North Carolina) who mistook them for Union troops. Having given the usual challenge, 'Halt! Who goes there?' the Carolina regiment seem to have opened fire before getting any coherent response. Jackson was shot three times, twice in the left arm and once in the right hand, but did not seem in imminent danger. In the melee, however, he could not get immediate medical attention, nor did being dropped by his stretcher bearers particularly help matters. Eventually Jackson was treated by doctors, having his left arm amputated, but pneumonia had already set in. He died from complications of this on 10 May.

2

Surprise, Surprise!

Old age is the most unexpected of all things that happen to a man.

Leon Trotsky, *Diary in Exile* (1959), 8 May 1935

Who was Miss Canary Islands 1936?

In the run-up to the Spanish Civil War, General Franco had been sent to a military command on the Canary Islands, mainly to get him out of the way as the government was suspicious that a Nationalist uprising might be on the cards. At this time Franco did indeed come into contact with the conspirators who were planning the revolution that would eventually sweep him to power, but he remained ambiguous about his support for it. Whilst tacitly going along with the plans being made in the spring and early summer of 1936, he was also writing to the government offering to help suppress Nationalistic unrest in the army. By June the Nationalist leaders, José Sanjurjo and Emilio Mola, had set a date for the rising, 18 July, which, they informed Franco, would happen with or without him. It was at this time, as he continued to vacillate, that the Nationalist high command gave him the nickname 'Miss Canary Islands 1936'. Nevertheless, it would not be a title he would hold for long. When the rebellion broke out a day early, Franco seized control of the Canary Islands before flying to Spanish Morocco to take command of the Army of Africa. The quick coup that they had hoped for was botched, however, and a civil war ensued. At the end of it one man would have supreme power – Miss Canary Islands 1936: Francisco Franco.

What was the star attraction at the Bronx Zoo in 1906?

The story of Ota Benga is one of the darkest episodes in the history of black America. Born in the Congo in 1883 during the savage personal rule of King Leopold II of Belgium, he was 'discovered' by the American missionary, Samuel Verner, who found him hiding amongst the Batwa people after Belgian agents had murdered his family. Verner had been sent to the country to look for pygmy specimens to display at the World's Fair in St Louis as part of the craze for 'ethnological expositions' in which 'primitive' peoples were displayed in mock-ups of their own villages. In Ota Benga he found just what he was looking for. Brought back to America, Benga was displayed in the 'University of Man' exhibit at the 1904 fair along with Inuit, Filipinos, Japanese tribal peoples, Zulus and, the star of the show, the native American, Geronimo, who was labelled 'The Human Tiger'.

After the fair Verner returned all his human exhibits to Africa but Ota Benga found difficulty in returning to his former life, particularly as many of the Batwa he had previously known had been massacred in his absence. After a few months he asked Verner whether he could return to the USA with him and Verner agreed. Back in the USA, Verner seemed unsure what to do with Ota Benga until it was suggested that he could become a living mascot for the American Museum of Natural History. The museum provided him with a white suit and engaged him to make small talk with visitors. For a brief moment he became a high-society celebrity until an incident when he threw a chair at Florence Guggenheim brought the headline in the *New York Times*, 'Benga Tries to Kill!' and his immediate dismissal.

It was now that Verner took Benga to the Bronx Zoo where initially he was allowed to roam the exhibits and help to feed the animals. It was not long, however, before it became clear that the zoo didn't see Benga as an employee but as an exhibit. He was first asked to hang his hammock in the monkey house and then, on 8 September 1906, a sign went up describing the zoo's newest acquisition, an African pygmy called Ota Benga. Some 40,000 people are estimated to have come to see the man now variously described as an elf, a cannibal, a dwarf and a savage, before a group of African-American ministers mounted a successful press campaign to end the spectacle.

Ota Benga was then moved to the Howard Colored Orphan Asylum where he was taught English and Scripture. Once it was considered that he had learnt all he could, his ritually filed teeth were capped and he was sent to Lynchburg, Virginia, under a new name, Otto Bingo, where he worked in a tobacco factory. Although this was better treatment than he had received in New York, Benga found it hard to settle into his new life and became depressed when he realised that he could never save enough money to return to Africa. On 20 March 1916 he took a friend's pistol and shot himself through the heart. He is buried in an unmarked grave.

Which monument was bought as a birthday present?

There are many types of stone that a man might buy his wife for her birthday but Sir Cecil Chubb, the self-made son of a saddler, wanted something a bit special. The stone, or rather stones, that he intended to purchase had an ancient history although no one was quite sure who had originally owned them. They had certainly belonged to the nuns of Amesbury Abbey before the Dissolution of the Monasteries and after that they came into a number of noble hands, including those of the Duke of Somerset and the Marquess of Queensberry, before finding their way into the Antrobus family. The Antrobuses held on to these treasures right up until the First World War. Then, tragically, in the opening months of the war, Edmund Antrobus, the heir to the family fortune, was killed and his father decided to sell up. Messrs Knight Frank and Rutley were called in to catalogue and sell the whole estate. It was into this auction, in the Palace Theatre in Salisbury, that Cecil Chubb walked on 21 September 1915. Shortly after, he emerged some £6,600 pounds poorer but the proud possessor of a unique birthday present for his wife – Lot 15: Stonehenge with about thirty acres, two rods and thirty-seven perches of adjoining downland.

Chubb later admitted that he had had no intention of buying the monument when he went into the sale but thought that, as a local boy made good (he was the owner of a successful asylum and several racehorses), perhaps he ought to buy it. Three years later he, or rather his wife, formally gave the monument to the nation on the condition that the gate money should go to the Red Cross for the duration of the war and that the people of local parishes should be able to visit for free, which they still can. The following year Chubb was created a baronet and took as his arms one of the distinctive trilithons of Stonehenge.

What was Oliver Cromwell's name?

Oliver Cromwell could have called himself many things, perhaps the least likely of which was Oliver Cromwell. He was a descendant of a Welshman, Morgan ap Williams, so if he had used the Welsh form of his surname he should have been 'Oliver son of Robert (his father)' or Oliver ap Robert. Instead he kept the family name of his great-great-grandmother, Catherine Cromwell, who had married the Welshman. But if we allow that this marriage formed a new Anglo-Welsh family, Oliver's real surname should have been Williams. So how did all this confusion come about?

Catherine Cromwell was born around 1483 and was the older sister of Tudor statesman Thomas Cromwell. Despite marrying into the Tudor line, she and her descendants chose to keep the Cromwell name and there are two theories as to why this might be. One states simply that the family wished to maintain their connection with their illustrious Tudor ancestor Thomas, even though that passed down only on the female side. However, it might also have been to disguise the male side of the family's heritage. This, rather embarrassingly for a republican like Oliver, connected them to the houses of Tudor, de Valois and Wittelsbach: the three royal dynasties of

England, France and the Holy Roman Empire respectively. This may seem unlikely but it is easily explained.

Cromwell's alleged paternal ancestor, Jasper Tudor, was the uncle of Henry VII of England. Both Jasper Tudor and his brother Edmund were sons of Owen Tudor and Catherine of Valois, daughter of the slightly inflammable Charles VI of France and the unfortunate Isabeau of Bavaria. Catherine was also the widow of Henry V of England. Her mother, Isabeau, was the daughter of Stephen III, Duke of Bavaria-Ingolstadt and Thaddea Visconti.

Interestingly after the Restoration, when it was not a good idea to be seen to have close links with Oliver Cromwell, some members of the family reverted for a time to calling themselves Williams.

Who gave all three of his sons the same name?

Karl I Alexander, Duke of Württemberg, fought under Prince Eugène of Savoy in the War of the Spanish Succession (1701–14), a spat that started over who should succeed to the Spanish throne after the death of the last Habsburg king. However, it rapidly mushroomed into an attempt by the Holy Roman Empire, England and the Dutch to prevent the crowns of Spain and France from uniting. It was in this war that the Duke of Marlborough made his name in England and Prince Eugène of Savoy made his in Austria. Karl Alexander was therefore delighted to serve with the illustrious prince. So impressed, indeed, was Karl with his military commander that he named all three of his sons Eugène (or rather Eugen in German). Whilst giving more than one child the same name was not unusual if one had died in childhood, all Karl's boys survived. Fortunately he had also given them other names – Karl, Friedrich and Ludwig – so everyone knew where they stood.

3

Men of the Cloth

It's great being a priest, isn't it, Ted?

Graham Linehan and Arthur Mathews, *Good Luck, Father Ted*
(1994), episode from the series *Father Ted*

Whom did Edward Gibbon accuse of piracy, murder, rape, sodomy and incest?

These were Edward Gibbon's comments in his *Decline and Fall of the Roman Empire* on the man who called himself Pope John XXIII and who is today known by the Catholic Church as Antipope John XXIII.

The distinction here between antipope and pope is important as there is also a Pope John XXIII who held the Holy See from 1958 to 1963. When he became pope there was some question as to whether he might take the title John XXIV to avoid any association with Gibbon's murderous pirate but he announced that he would be Pope John XXIII in order to make it clear that the murderous pirate was not a proper pope and so the number twenty-three was still available. Interestingly enough, he could also have chosen to be Pope John XX as, due to a clerical error, no Pope John ever had that number.

So what did Antipope John XXIII do to get such a bad press? Well, partly it was a matter of politics. John was one of three people claiming to be pope in the early fifteenth century during the split known as 'The Great Schism', each of whom had the support of a few cardinals and, most importantly of all, that of one or more of the European rulers who really held the power. John was certainly a little worldly, having managed a stint as a pirate and run a protection racket at the University of Bologna before deciding to become religious. In fact at the time of his 'election' as pope, he wasn't even a priest and had to be ordained quickly before he could be enthroned. But in many ways he was no worse than the others – just wholly unsuitable as pope.

Eventually everyone in Europe got rather tired of all these popes who kept popping up and a council was called at Constance between 1414 and 1417, which decided to get rid of all the current popes and antipopes. Gregory XII saw which way the wind was blowing and retired gracefully; Benedict XIII retreated to Spain, still claiming it was really unfair; but John XXIII ran away, only to get caught and dragged back before the Council. The charges brought before him at the Council, as described by Gibbon, were certainly exaggerated but they had enough of a ring of truth about them to ensure his deposition and imprisonment. Once the Council had agreed on a new pope, Martin V, everyone felt a little more forgiving, however, and John, now just plain old Baldassarre Cossa, was released. This was a good result for the antipope really, since he had been charged with nearly every major crime in existence and was sentenced to a mere three years in prison. Jan Hus, who was also condemned at Constance, had agreed to recant all the theological statements he had made if they could be proved wrong and they burnt him at the stake anyway. After his release the former antipope was made Cardinal Bishop of Tusculum by Martin V and moved to Florence, where he died in 1419. Cosimo de Medici, a big patron of the arts, commissioned Donatello and Michelozzi to prepare a magnificent tomb for him, which survives to this day.

Which famous monk married a nun?

In the mediaeval period the marriage of monks or nuns, let alone one to the other, was generally frowned upon. Even popes hadn't taken wives since the time of Adrian II in the ninth century (although a few of the less reliable popes had taken a mistress or two and some were possibly even secretly married). All marital prospects therefore suddenly declined for one young man returning from the University of Erfurt who was struck by lightning. According to his own testimony he immediately shouted, 'Help, St Anna, I will become a monk,' and was immediately as good as his word.

Martin Luther wasn't going to be a normal monk, however. His own personal devotion didn't tally with the apparent venality of the

Church, evidence of which he now saw all around him, leading him to write to the archbishop of Mainz and Magdeburg, complaining about the sale of indulgences and attaching his ninety-five theses (which, legend has it, he also handily nailed to the door of the castle church in Wittenberg the same day). The archbishop was at the time using part of the money from indulgence sales to pay off his bribery debts so he wasn't best pleased about Luther's complaints. He had the theses checked for heresy and sent the lot off to the pope without bothering to reply. One thing led to another and, before you knew it, Luther had been excommunicated and outlawed, and the Reformation had kicked off.

By now Luther was getting regular requests from nuns who wanted to escape from their nunneries. On 7 April 1523 a group of nine of these escapees arrived at Luther's home, having been smuggled out of the Cistercian monastery of Nimbschen in herring barrels. Amongst them was Katharina von Bora. The other eight ex-nuns were soon married to locals in Wittenberg but Katharina let it be known that she wanted to marry Luther himself. He was initially reluctant, taking the view that, as an excommunicant and outlaw, he wouldn't make an ideal husband. She prevailed, however, and he married the woman he would later fondly call 'My Lord Katie' on 13 June 1525. They had six children – three girls and three boys – and lived in 'the Black Cloister', a former Augustinian monastery in Wittenberg, which the Elector gave them as a wedding present.

Who cremated Jesus Christ?

Dr William Price was an unusual man by the standards of late nineteenth-century Wales. In an age of fervent Christian belief, Price claimed to be the reincarnation of a Celtic priest who had died some 10,000 years before. In other words, a druid.

This was in itself enough to enrage many a decent chapel-goer but it was not this that would get Price into trouble. Nor was it his assertion that the ancient Welsh (and the modern ones too if he could persuade them) enjoyed open marriages, naked sunbathing and vegetarianism. It was not even his habit of carrying a stick marked with arcane Greek insignia and topped with a crescent moon, or the fox skin that he always wore on his head – with the animal's head still attached. What enraged the public of 1883 has today become part of everyday life.

William Price had a son who, not surprisingly for someone as eccentric as himself, he had christened Jesus Christ. There was nothing to actually stop him using that name although it probably made the poor boy's life a bit difficult.

The real problems for William Price and Jesus Christ only came after Jesus' death. When Jesus died William refused to register the death. Instead he took his son's body to a nearby field where he built a huge bonfire. This attracted quite a lot of local attention and a fair few people came to see what he was up to. When they saw him put his son's body on the bonfire and set light to it, there was a riot.

In late nineteenth-century Britain the dead were always buried. The thought of burning them horrified the gathered crowd. They surged past Price towards the flames and pulled the charred body from the pyre. The police were called. William was arrested and charged with burning a body in an attempt to prevent an inquest.

But it was a flawed prosecution. Nobody had claimed that William was burning the body to hide evidence of wrong-doing. His son had died under perfectly normal circumstances. In court his barrister argued that there was no law to say that a body had to be buried, not cremated, and he was quite right. At the time people thought that burial alone was decent but no law existed to prevent any other means of disposing of the dead. So William Price walked free, fox-skin hat and all. When he died nine years later at the ripe old age of ninety-one he was, of course, cremated. Nearly 20,000 people came to watch. He'd started a fashion. Four years after his death Britain's first crematorium was opened. Today seven out of ten bodies are cremated instead of buried – though not usually in open fields. William Price's most eccentric idea has become the normal way of doing things.

Who made 200 monks jump?

Jean-Antoine Nollet was trained for the religious life, which is why he generally liked to be known as Abbé Nollet, and as such could probably have made any number of monks jump whenever he chose, but what he really wanted to do was demonstrate an important scientific point. Although nominally a man of the cloth, Nollet was also a great scientist with a particular interest in the strange phenomenon of electricity that, at the beginning of the eighteenth century, still hadn't been properly explained. In 1745 he developed the theory of electrical attraction and repulsion, which he thought came from there being two types of electricity – positive and negative. This brought him into direct conflict with Benjamin Franklin, founding father of the USA and extreme kite flyer, whose ideas would eventually supplant his own.

What Nollet and Franklin had in common, however, was the ability to turn an experiment into a great show. Whilst Franklin flew kites in electrical storms to prove that lightning was electrical (and still found time to invent a flexible urinary catheter), Nollet had developed an amusing way of showing how electrical conductivity worked. Having been appointed Preceptor in Natural Philosophy to the royal family, he was required to demonstrate physics experiments for the education and amusement of King Louis XV and his entourage. At Versailles in 1746 he persuaded 180 royal guards to line up whilst he connected them together with a thin wire. He then attached each end of the line to a Leyden jar. This was an early form of capacitor, which stored an electrical charge. When the unfortunate soldiers at the end of the line were attached to it, the electricity discharged through them via the whole line, making all the soldiers jump in the air. This demonstration of the action of electricity on human bodies greatly amused the royal party but also made an important point.

Nollet had greater ambitions and back in Paris he used his ecclesiastical authority to arrange a yet more spectacular public demonstration in the hope of discovering the speed of electrical transmission. For this he summoned 200 (some sources say over 1,000) monks from the Carthusian Grand Convent in Paris whom he placed in a line over a mile long, all connected together by iron wires twenty-five feet long. Nollet then attached a series of large Leyden jars to one end of the line and discharged them, sending a few hundred volts through the unsuspecting monastic daisy chain. Apparently instantaneously, all the monks jumped in the air, shouting and cursing with the same force, suggesting to Nollet that electricity passes instantaneously and can travel over long distances. This experiment has since been claimed as the origin of the telegraph.

How old was the youngest pope?

It's not easy to find out how old some of the earlier popes were at the time of their election as there was little in the way of good birth records. A claim is often made that Benedict IX became pope at the tender age of eleven but that calculation is based on the fact that we have absolutely no idea when he was born. The more sober *Catholic Encyclopaedia* estimates that he was around twenty, which seems more likely. If so, he is beaten to the title of youngest pontiff by John XII who was certainly only eighteen when he got the top job. What both popes have in common is that they got the post through nepotism and they were both wholly unsuited to the role. In his splendidly vitriolic *Book of Gomorrah*, St Peter Damian accused Benedict of being a homosexual devil who practised bestiality. Whilst this might be going a bit too far, Benedict certainly managed to be pope three times (having been kicked out twice), was probably married and once sold the papacy to his godfather.

John XII wasn't much better. He was accused of invoking demons whilst playing dice, toasting the devil with wine, and sleeping with scores of women, including his father's concubine and his own niece. He was also accused of murders, blindings and of ordaining a ten-year-old as a bishop. He died aged twenty-seven, possibly killed by the irate husband of one of his lovers – a fate he shared with Pope Benedict VII.

4

Heads

So the heart be right, it is no matter which way the head lies.

Sir Walter Raleigh (at his execution, on being asked which way he preferred to lay his head)

What did Walter Raleigh's wife keep in her handbag?

The story of Sir Walter Raleigh is one of fortunes both won and lost. He was for a time the epitome of the Elizabethan court – daring and dazzling, a rich adventurer with the ear of the queen and the hand of one of her ladies. But on Elizabeth's death his fortunes and those of his wife, Bess, began to change. In the new Stuart era he was considered something of a throwback, a flamboyant and annoying reminder of the old century. Getting rid of him proved all too easy for King James and his followers who hated the old explorer. Raleigh was arrested and tried as a conspirator in a planned Catholic uprising known as the Main Plot. He was found guilty (although on pathetic evidence, even by those days' standards), sentenced to death and sent to the Tower where he stayed until 1616. In that year he was released on condition that he search for the second time for El Dorado – the fabled City of Gold. Raleigh set off for Guiana. Here the endgame began to play out. Off the South American coast Raleigh's men, against his orders, attacked the Spanish outpost of San Thome during which his son Wat was shot dead. On his return there was worse to come. Not only had he not found El Dorado but the Spanish ambassador was furious about the attack, as England and Spain had now signed a peace treaty. The ambassador insisted the original death sentence on Raleigh from 1603 be reinstated and King James agreed.

Raleigh was beheaded on 29 October 1618 and his body was buried in St Margaret's church (next to Westminster Abbey). His head, however, was not. As was the custom, this was embalmed and given to his wife as a sort of grisly memento. Bess seemed rather fond of it, however, and from then on carried it around everywhere with her in a red bag. It was reported that when people came to the family home she would even ask them whether they would like to see Walter, at which point she would produce the bag with the head in it. For all this eccentricity, Bess spent the best part of the next thirty years vigorously pressing for the rehabilitation of her husband's reputation and, in the process, helped to undermine the Stuart monarchy in the run-up to the Civil War. By the time of her own death around 1647 her lobbying (and his head) had helped to make Raleigh a hero again. The head was then passed to Raleigh's son and was finally buried in his grave with him in London in 1668.

Who hung the world's most famous painting in his bathroom?

Francis I of France wanted nothing more than to be the perfect Renaissance monarch and in many ways he was. As a great patron of the arts it was Francis who invited the aged Leonardo da Vinci to leave Italy and come to join him at his chateau at Amboise in 1516. It was a good deal for da Vinci – the offer of a manor house close to the chateau and very generous terms for himself and his staff – and so he accepted.

Amongst the possessions that he carried over the Alps to France with him was a particular painting, a mysterious piece for which there is no record of the commission, no name for the sitter and not even a signature – the *Mona Lisa*. It remains unclear why da Vinci had kept it instead of giving it to whoever had commissioned it (assuming that it was, like most portraits, a commission) but once in France he did agree to sell it to Francis I. The French king first hung the portrait in the chateau at Amboise before moving it, with his court, first to Fontainebleau and then to Paris. In Paris, this small and at the time not well-known work had to vie with many other paintings in what would become the Louvre art collection. Because the king's palace walls were over-crowded it was hung in a bathroom.

There the *Mona Lisa* remained until Louis XIV moved it, together with his whole court, to the newly built palace of Versailles. His son, Louis XV, disliked the painting and had it sent back to

Paris, where it stayed until Napoleon Bonaparte declared himself emperor. He rather liked the painting and had it hung in his bedroom, where it took pride of place until he was removed from office, when it went back to the Louvre.

The painting's last journey took place in 1911 when an Italian house painter called Vincenzo Peruggia managed to steal it, believing it to have been illegally taken from Italy by the Duke of Wellington's least-favourite relative, Napoleon, which it hadn't. He returned the painting to the place it had originated from, Florence, where he tried to sell it to an art dealer and, as might be expected, was instantly arrested. The painting did not immediately return to France, however, but toured Italy first. This was no great loss to the Louvre, which, surprisingly, had seen ticket sales increase in the two years that the painting was missing. This was because more people paid to come and see the spot where the *Mona Lisa* was stolen from than had come to see the masterpiece itself.

How did one man's ear start a war?

The 1729 Treaty of Seville allowed for Spanish coastguards to board British ships in the Caribbean to check whether they were breaking the terms of the treaty, which forbade trading with Spanish colonies. So it was that on 9 April 1731 a Spanish boarding party came alongside the brig *Rebecca* just off Havana, as she made for Jamaica. The Spanish coastguard clearly believed that the *Rebecca* was carrying contraband but her captain, Robert Jenkins, denied this. According to Jenkins, the Spanish began physically abusing him to try to get him to tell them where the loot was. He was half strangled and beaten up. Then the Spanish commander cut off a part of his ear, 'bidding him to carry it to his Master King George'. The ship was plundered and sabotaged with the intent, so the Royal Navy claimed, of ensuring that she would never make it back to port. Miraculously the *Rebecca* did survive, however, bringing back home to England the beaten, bruised and partially earless Jenkins in June of that year.

Whilst there was some sympathy for Jenkins at the time, and representations were made to the Spanish authorities about this and other alleged cases of Spanish intimidation, no real action was taken until 1738. By then Britain's relations with Spain had soured further and Jenkins' mutilation provided the perfect rallying point for anti-Spanish sentiment. Jenkins was called to attend a House of Commons Committee examining Spanish predations. According to one version of the story, he turned up brandishing his now famous ear, which he had pickled and put in a jar. Sadly there's no independent evidence that he even attended the committee, let alone that he brought his ear with him. The following year, the political opposition to Robert Walpole's government, which had used Jenkins' ear as a symbol of Spanish aggression and cruelty, finally got their way and war was declared on Spain.

The fighting in what became known as the War of Jenkins' Ear took place in the Caribbean, culminating in the successful British capture of Puerto Bello in Panama, in recognition of which Portobello Road in London was named. The British admiral in charge of the expedition, Admiral Vernon, was also a great navy moderniser. His insistence on watering down the rum ration so that his sailors were sober enough to sail, and his habit of always wearing an old grogram coat, gave the world the term grog for watered-down rum. By 1742 the war, although still being fought, had become no more than a sideshow in the War of the Austrian Succession, which was by then raging in Europe, engulfing Spain, Britain, France, Russia and the Holy Roman Empire.

Which general gave his name to facial hair?

General Ambrose Everett Burnside was not, by his own admission, one of the best Union Army generals. If he had a failing it was that he was remarkably amiable and easily befriended those around him, which made him very popular. This, and his impressive physical appearance, led to his rapid rise through the ranks of the Union Army during the American Civil War, leaving him in a position of command that he didn't want and wasn't, frankly, very well suited to. Twice he refused the command of the Army of the Potomac and only took it on the third occasion when he was ordered to do so. The most common comment after one of his engagements was that he had dithered and failed to press home an advantage, committing his troops piecemeal rather than in a concerted assault. After the Battle of the Crater, and a previous disastrous defeat at Fredericksburg, Burnside was finally relieved of his command.

Burnside's contribution to the American Civil War would not seem to amount to much, were it not for one other distinguishing feature. Throughout the conflict he wore a unique arrangement of facial hair, with a thick moustache and bearded cheeks, but a clean-shaven chin, the inverse of another American style, the goatee. Despite his failings as a general, Burnside remained very popular after the war, and both his style of facial hair, and his distinctive soft hat, became known as burnsides. The popularity of the hat soon waned and, as time went on, the association weakened between Burnside and the arrangement of facial hair. At some point in the late nineteenth century the name became transposed as sideburns, which perhaps was considered to make more sense, and so the term was born.

Which English king breathed fire then expired?

On Thursday, 2 August 1100, King William II of England, known as 'Rufus' thanks to his ruddy complexion, was at a hunting lodge in the New Forest, probably near to Brockenhurst. With him was his brother Henry, Robert fitz Haimo and Walter Tirel. For some reason they had not left the lodge that morning to hunt but remained there until after lunch.

William of Malmesbury says in his chronicle that a foreign monk had come to the lodge before sunrise that morning and had spoken to Robert fitz Haimo. The monk had told him of his dream the previous night in which he had seen the king enter a small church and, with his usual disdain, sneer at the congregation. He had then approached the cross and, seizing it, began to gnaw at its arms. The cross had suffered this for a time and had then kicked William to the floor. As the king hit the ground he had belched fire at the cross, the billowing smoke from his mouth reaching so high as to nearly touch the stars.

This may have seemed a touch alarming and fitz Haimo certainly urged the king not to hunt that morning. Such warnings, visions and dreams were common, however, particularly amongst wishful-thinking clerics who wanted to see an end to the reign of the decidedly ungodly William. Knowing this, the king rarely took note of these warnings, so it is more likely that urgent business that morning kept him from the forest, or perhaps just a hangover, for he had indulged more fully than usual at the previous evening's meal. The chronicler Ordericus Vitalis says that both William and Walter Tirel poured scorn on the warning and, on hearing of the foreign monk's dream, relayed through fitz Haimo, William is reported to have said: *'He is a monk and to get money dreams like a monk.'*

It was late afternoon by the time the hunting party left the lodge. In the woods the party dispersed, as was usual, to their various positions. William stayed close by his friend Walter Tirel, Lord of Poix. In the early-evening light, beaters were set to flush out the deer, which would be chased past fixed positions, known as trysts, from where the hunters would shoot, dismounted, with crossbows or longbows. In two of these positions stood King William and Walter Tirel. The sun was sinking lower and the shadows lengthening, making it harder to aim. To the east the forest lay in deep shadow, whilst to the west the hunters were squinting into the setting sun. Suddenly two stags broke from cover and the cry was raised.

There is some confusion as to what happened next. William of Malmesbury says the king took aim and fired, but the arrow passed over the animal's back, only grazing it. The startled beast darted away but Walter Tirel already had the second animal in his sights and loosed an arrow as it ran between him and the king. Again the arrow failed to hit its mark but sped over the stag's back and on towards the king. William had no time to move and the dart plunged into his chest, piercing his heart. Stunned, he broke off the shaft of the arrow, thereby hastening his own death, and fell to the ground without uttering a single word. Within seconds he was dead.

5

What's in a Name?

Three things I never lends – my 'oss, my wife, and my name.

R. S. Surtees, *Hillingdon Hall* (1845), chapter 33

Who was Gordon Bennett?

James Gordon Bennett Junior was born to the good life, having inherited the *New York Herald* newspaper from his father and founded the *International Herald Tribune*. To say that he was a flamboyant character would be an understatement. To improve the sales of his paper he took to underwriting heroic expeditions and sponsoring epic events. It was Gordon Bennett who paid for Henry Morton Stanley to go to Africa in search of David Livingstone (in return for exclusive coverage) as well as funding George Washington De Long's fatal expedition to the North Pole in 1881. In the sports arena Bennett sponsored 'Gordon Bennett' cups in yacht and motor racing, in addition to the world's oldest race for gas-filled balloons (if we exclude the business in Paris in 1870), the Coupe Aéronautique Gordon Bennett. He also introduced polo to the USA.

Bennett's personal life was no less exciting or unusual. In 1866 he had won the first ever transatlantic yacht race but it was an unfortunate incident in 1877 that perhaps, above all others, turned Bennett's name into an exclamation. In that year he became engaged to the New York socialite and heiress Caroline May, whose parents had gathered together a $20,000 trousseau for her – the largest ever assembled at that time. At a cocktail party at the May mansion, however, Bennett arrived late and very drunk. Mistaking a large fireplace for a urinal, he proceeded to relieve himself, in public, in front of his prospective in-laws and their guests, leaving both the fire and his fiancée's ardour thoroughly doused. Shortly after this, the engagement was cancelled and Bennett found himself on the wrong end of a public horsewhipping, administered by the aggrieved girl's brother. This extraordinary event, startling even by Bennett's standards, turned his name into an expression of surprise – Gordon Bennett!

Shortly after the incident Bennett himself decided to take prolonged leave from New York and headed to Europe to avoid further encounters with vengeful siblings. He would not attempt marriage again until he was seventy-three years old when he wedded the heiress of the Reuter's news agency fortune.

Who is the Bob in 'Bob's your uncle'?

Lord Robert Cecil, 3rd Marquess of Salisbury, was three times Prime Minister and, like many aristocratic politicians of his era, was not afraid of promoting members of his family to positions of power.

The origin of the phrase 'Bob's your uncle' comes from one such promotion when, in 1887, he promoted his nephew Arthur Balfour to the position of Irish Secretary in the hope that Balfour might put down the Irish rebels in the same way that he had suppressed the truculent crofters of Skye when he was at the Scottish Office. This move saw Cecil christened 'Uncle Bob' by some newspapers and so the term 'Bob's your uncle' emerged as a way of describing how simple it was for relatives of the great marquess to get jobs in government. None of this actually bothered the larger-than-life Cecil and in 1895 he appointed another nephew, Balfour's brother, Chief Secretary for Ireland. By 1900, his eldest son, three nephews and a son-in-law were all in government positions.

When he retired, his health damaged by his corpulence and his habit of only taking short rides on a tricycle for exercise, the role of Prime Minister was taken by his nephew Arthur, keeping the government very much in the family.

Who was the first nosy parker?

The original Nosy Parker was, according to Corpus Christi College, Cambridge, their former master and archbishop of Canterbury,

Matthew Parker. Parker had been chaplain to Henry VIII and Anne Boleyn, and had hence taught the future Queen Elizabeth. On her accession to the throne she rewarded him with the post of archbishop of Canterbury, with responsibility for trying to create some sort of settlement between the new Anglican Church and the old Catholic faith. Frankly, this was a pretty tricky job, what with a small number of Catholics at one extreme plotting to kill Elizabeth and the ultra-Protestant 'precisians' at the other, who wouldn't have minded getting rid of every Catholic in the realm. Parker attacked this problem by trying to find a reasonable, logical basis for the new Anglican faith. Between 1563 and 1568 he produced a new version of the Bible, which remained the official text until James I's Authorised Version. He also took Cranmer's slightly rambling forty-two doctrines of the Church of England and turned them into the much neater thirty-nine Articles of Religion, which still form the basis of Anglican doctrine to this day.

Furthermore Parker wanted to prove that the origins of the Church in England were independent of Rome, as this would provide a neat justification for the English Reformation: the Church hadn't suddenly declared itself independent; it always had been autonomous and was just throwing off an imposed foreign influence. And it was in going about trying to demonstrate this that Parker became 'Nosy Parker'.

He managed to persuade the Privy Council to issue him with a warrant to 'make a general search after all such records and muniments as related to these Realms, and which upon the dissolution of the monasteries had fallen into private hands'.

And there were an awful lot of these records lying around. Every monastery had once had a library and muniment room where it kept the deeds and charters that granted it its lands and privileges. When the monasteries had been dissolved these had generally come on the open market, some being sold, some lost and some just bundled up and thrown in a cupboard. Mixed up with the legal documents, however, were other works – indeed, some of the most important works of history and literature that England possesses. They included illuminated manuscripts, original chronicles, heroic poetry, mediaeval laws – the whole literary corpus from the Anglo-Saxon Chronicle to Zosimus.

In searching for his proof of an independent English Church, Parker came across all this material and realised that perhaps the nation's greatest treasure was teetering on the brink of destruction. He therefore assiduously searched for and acquired every document, charter, chronicle and poem he could find, gaining him the title 'Nosy Parker'.

On his death he left to his old college one of the greatest manuscript libraries in the world and, in doing so, preserved a thousand years of British history and literature that might otherwise have been lost. Not that the nation was terribly grateful. He died in 1575 and was buried at Lambeth but during the Civil War his remains were exhumed and thrown on a dung heap.

Who formed the first lynch mob?

Several theories have been put forward for the origin of the term lynching but it seems most probably to come from Captain William Lynch, a Virginian planter and local Justice. During the American War of Independence, Virginia was a dangerous place for independent-minded settlers to live. Following a strike by Welsh miners the rumour began spreading of a pro-British uprising against the settlers of south-western Virginia and in response William Lynch, together with other prominent Justices and military officers, began rounding up suspects and subjecting them to ad hoc trials at which they sat in judgment without reference to any other authority. Those found guilty of treachery were either whipped or conscripted into the revolutionary army. Two years later, on 24 December 1782, the General Assembly of Virginia passed an Act that named Lynch and three other leading members of these irregular courts, and retrospectively legitimised their actions in what became known as Lynch's Law. Within Lynch's lifetime, the term 'lynch law' was already in use although, interestingly, neither Lynch nor his compatriots ever executed an individual and the term lynching, to mean an extra-legal hanging, was used only after his death.

6

Animal Magic

Man is the Only Animal that Blushes. Or needs to.

Mark Twain, *Following the Equator* (1897), chapter 27

What was the Battle of the Herrings?

The Battle of the Herrings took place on 12 February 1429 when Sir John Fastolf (who is one of the models for Shakespeare's Falstaff) was on a mercy mission to relieve the English besiegers of Orléans. With Lent fast approaching, the English army was in danger of starving, not because there was any real food shortage but because eating meat was banned during that season. An army marches on its stomach, as Napoleon once said, and if the siege was to be maintained the soldiers would have to have another source of protein. That was why Sir John and his men were valiantly battling towards Orléans with a supply column of herrings.

Just outside Rouvray the herrings found themselves in trouble, however. To the south-west a much larger combined French and Scottish army had appeared and it began a ferocious cannon bombardment that cut a swathe through the English soldiers and their fish whilst staying out of range of the English archers. Just as all seemed lost the French allies from Scotland made an error and John Stewart of Darnley managed to seize defeat from the jaws of victory. Ignoring orders from his French superiors, he told his men to dismount and attack the herring carts but as soon as they were in range of the English longbowmen they were, not surprisingly, mown down. Desperate to regain the initiative, the French commander then sent in his men-at-arms to support them and they too were felled, much as they had been at Agincourt. Fastolf, seeing an opening, then sent his small band of men-at-arms into the fray and put the French and Scots into full retreat. Now unopposed, he marched on to the outskirts of Orléans where it was fish suppers all round.

This peculiar scrap between the English, Scots and French over a few barrels of herrings had unexpected ramifications. In the short term, the French army, which was meant to be raising the siege instead of attacking herring carts, was routed. It was also on that same day that another French leader was begging the high command for a chance to attack the English at Orléans. They had until this point been reluctant as this particular commander was a bit unusual. Now with news of the defeat at the Battle of the Herrings drifting into camp, they decided to let this individual have a go. So Joan of Arc got her chance to raise the siege of Orléans, which she did, in the process becoming one of France's greatest heroines.

Who were the victims of the War of the Currents?

The War of the Currents was fought in the late nineteenth and early twentieth centuries between the companies of George Westinghouse Junior and Thomas Edison. In the race to provide America with electric lighting, two methods of transmission had been proposed, the 110-volt direct current model of Edison, and Westinghouse's alternating current, which used 3,000 volts. Westinghouse's AC system had the advantage of losing less power in transmission, as transformers could be used to step up the voltage for distribution and then bring it back down for public consumption, but Edison believed that this high-voltage transmission was dangerous.

Already losing the War of the Currents due to the failure of his DC system to deliver power over distances greater than about a mile without significant voltage drop, Edison set about a publicity campaign to persuade the public that AC was too dangerous to adopt. To do this he presided over a number of public electrocutions of stray cats and dogs until in 1903 the chance came to make a really big statement. That year Topsy, a circus elephant that had killed three people, was ordered to be put down. The American Society for the Prevention of Cruelty to Animals considered hanging to be too cruel and so Edison offered to electrocute the beast. The *Commercial Advertiser* of New York carried the story on Monday, 5 January 1903.

> Topsy, the ill-tempered Coney Island elephant, was put to death in Luna Park, Coney Island, yesterday afternoon. The execution was witnessed by 1,500 or more curious persons, who went down to the island to see the end of the huge beast, to whom they had fed peanuts and cakes in summers that are gone. In order to make Topsy's execution quick and sure 460 grams of cyanide of potassium were fed to her in carrots. Then a hawser was put around her neck and one end attached to a donkey engine and the other to a post. Next wooden sandals lined with copper were attached to her feet. These electrodes were connected by copper wire with the Edison electric light plant and a current of 6,600 volts was sent through her body. The big beast died without a trumpet or a groan.

Edison filmed the event and even went as far as trying to persuade people to refer to electrocution as being 'Westinghoused' but, due to the physical limitations of the DC system, the War of the Currents was in fact already lost and Westinghouse was triumphant.

However, one macabre side-effect of the War of the Currents means that it is still claiming victims to this day. In his desire to discredit the AC system, Edison employed Harold P. Brown to develop the electric chair – an AC-based execution system for criminals, which he hoped would not only satisfy the American public's desire for a more humane form of execution but also discredit Westinghouse to boot.

It was first used on William Kemmler in 1890, utilising one of Westinghouse's own generators, which Edison had bought by subterfuge, supposedly for use in a university. The execution was botched and the initial 1,000-volt charge failed to kill Kemmler. He was then shocked again, this time with 2,000 volts, which caused blood vessels in his arms to burst and his body to catch fire. The whole event took eight minutes and was described by one witness as 'far worse than hanging'. Westinghouse is reported to have commented: 'They would have done better using an axe.' Despite this, both the electric chair and the AC system remained in use, much to Edison's annoyance.

What was unusual about Thomas Hobson's stable?

Thomas Hobson lived from about 1545 to 1631 and was the university carrier in Cambridge. In this role he served the university for over sixty years, making the regular coach – well, cart – journey between Cambridge and the Bull Inn in London, as well as keeping a livery stable opposite St Catherine's College where he rented out horses to locals and students.

The term 'Hobson's choice', which means an apparent choice where in fact there is none, comes from his method of allocating these horses. Many stables allowed the hirer to choose which horse they wanted but this could lead to the overuse of particularly fine or fast horses, which might shorten their useful lives. Hobson allowed his customers to choose whichever horse they wanted, provided it was the one nearest the stable door. In this manner he rotated his stock and prevented his best animals from being over-exploited.

After his death on 1 January 1631 at the age of eighty-six, a number of satirical poems began to appear about Hobson, including two by John Milton. His first, 'On the University Carrier who sickn'd in the time of his vacancy, being forbid to go to *London*, by reason of the Plague', jokingly imagines that the ancient Hobson would have continued to drive between London and Cambridge for ever had he not been temporarily banned from making the journey due to the plague in London. Being as a result at a loose end with nothing to do, it suggests, he promptly died.

Hobson was a shrewd businessman and 'Hobson's choice' helped him to amass a considerable fortune, including the site of the priory of Anglesey, assorted manors and numerous other properties in Cambridge and beyond. His daughters could therefore afford to marry well, one to a gentleman and the other to a baronet, although Hobson wryly noted that the marriage portions he had to pay for such grand matches left him 'whereby my estate is much lesse than heretofore it was'. He did, however, have enough to leave money in his will to improve the water conduit into Cambridge, which still exists today and now bears his name.

How did Dracula get his name?

Dracula got his name from a mythical beast, or rather his father's mythical beast. The man on whom at least part of the legend of Dracula is based is Vlad the Impaler, a fifteenth-century ruler of Wallachia (now a province of Romania). But the title originally belonged to his father, Vlad II, who was a vassal of the Hungarian Empire, responsible for protecting the trade routes from the south into Transylvania and beyond.

At the time when Vlad II was on the throne, Europe was threatened from the south by the expansion of the Ottoman Empire. Vlad therefore decided to curry favour with the Holy Roman Emperor in the hope of receiving help during any Ottoman invasion of his lands. To do this, Vlad took the oath of the Order of the Dragon in 1431 by which he promised to protect the emperor's family in return for the emperor's goodwill. Vlad was rather pleased about his induction into a high chivalric order and became known as Vlad the Dragon, or in his own language Vlad Dracul.

As is often the way, things did not go to plan for Vlad. When the Ottomans threatened, Hungary (which was part of the Holy Roman Empire) ordered Vlad to obey the Oath of the Dragon he had taken and join the crusade against the Turks. Vlad refused so, after the Christian army was destroyed, the Hungarians repaid the compliment by arranging to murder him and his eldest son (who was blinded with hot iron stakes and then buried alive). They then replaced them with their own nominee. Young Vlad was rather cross about this and decided to back the Ottomans, who invaded Wallachia and installed him as puppet ruler. The Hungarians certainly weren't having such nonsense, however, and promptly reinvaded to remove him. Vlad now wisely ran away to Moldavia but when a new sultan came to the Ottoman throne, whom he hated, he took a chance and fled to the Hungarian court, of all places. Astonishingly, the king was terribly impressed with Vlad's knowledge of things Ottoman and decided to pardon him. Reinstalled on the throne of Wallachia, he proudly took the title that his father had once held from the Hungarian court, calling himself Dracula – the son of the Dragon.

Who fought the Dog Tax War?

Just when you thought there simply couldn't be any more stupid wars, along comes the Dog Tax War. The name is a bit misleading as it wasn't really a war at all but more of a nasty colonial spat between the European settlers of New Zealand (not the New Zealand that Willem Janszoon discovered) and the native Maori people. It was, however, caused by a dog tax.

The Maori people had not had a good nineteenth century. In 1840, just before the beginnings of large-scale European settlement, they were a populous, independent nation, but by the outbreak of the Dog Tax War in 1889 they owned just 10 per cent of the least fertile areas of their land and their population had fallen by 90 per cent, mainly due to diseases introduced by the settlers. In this situation, strongly anti-settler groups had grown up amongst the Maori, as perhaps you might expect, and they were looking for an excuse to expel the Europeans.

In 1889 the white-led Hokianga County Council on North Island obliged when it imposed a tax of two shillings and sixpence on dog owners for every dog they owned. Not surprisingly, some people objected, notably the Maori people of the Waima area who refused to pay and were promptly arrested. Matters now began to get a bit heated as the Maori independence movement, the Pai Marire, got involved. When the only police officer for the region arrived in Waima on 28 April he found a well-armed group, refusing to pay their dog tax and threatening to advance on the administrative capital, Rawene. As the war party marched off he sent a message to Rawene, advising that all women and children be evacuated for fear of a massacre. Soon the entire town was empty. Meanwhile six policemen from Auckland had arrived to defend the town and had set up a cannon on the quay. Just what they expected to do with one cannon is unclear but when the angry Maori mob arrived, they wisely ran away.

At this point it looked as if a war might well be in the offing, were it not for the quick thinking of a local hotel owner (and the only remaining European in the whole town), Bob Cochrane. He opened his bar, invited the war party in and, rather than pointing cannons at them, offered them a beer and a chat. This calmed things down a bit. The war party (which only numbered about twenty people in the first place) then went home.

By now the government had had time to overreact and sent a force of some 120 heavily armed soldiers and policemen, plus a warship, to the area. Fearing an all-out firefight, the local member of the House of Representatives, Hone Heke, sent a telegram to the Maori leader, Hone Toia, advising him to disband his men and seek redress through parliament. This he did, but he and fifteen others were later arrested. In court Hone Toia pleaded not guilty to conspiring to levy war but guilty of conspiring to prevent the collection of taxes. He was sentenced to eighteen months' hard labour and, to add insult to injury, all his group had to pay their dog tax.

7

Bedhopping

I have never yet seen anyone whose desire to build up his
moral power was as strong as sexual desire.

Confucius (K'ung Fu-tzu), *Analects*, chapter 9, v. 17, trans.
Arthur Waley

How did Charles the Mad stop his wife having an affair?

Isabeau of Bavaria has gone down in history as a misguided nymphomaniac who signed away her son's inheritance. She was the daughter of Thaddea Visconti and Stephen III of Bavaria, and she married the unpromisingly monikered French king Charles the Mad in 1385 at one of the unhappiest periods in French history.

She had few abilities as a leader, and suffered from being both female and foreign at a time when such things didn't give you much authority at the French court. This proved problematic, particularly during Charles's bouts of insanity. She further compromised her position by becoming the mistress of Louis of Orléans, whilst her sexual appetite and financial incontinence made her extremely unpopular, particularly in Paris. Eventually the king, who had developed a persecution complex fixated on his wife, disbanded her court at the Hôtel Barbette, which was well known for its extravagance and promiscuity.

In 1417, the queen was banished, allegedly due to the behaviour of her ladies-in-waiting, but actually because the king believed her to have been having an affair with her *grand maître d'hôtel*, Louis de Bosredon. Louis was arrested and imprisoned. Later he was sewn into a leather sack that bore the legend, *Laissiez passer la justice du roy* ('May the king's justice be served') and thrown into the Seine. Isabeau's banishment may also have had much to do with her unpopularity at court, brought about by her rapacious behaviour, particularly her channelling of state funds to her Bavarian family.

After the defeat in 1415 of the French forces at Agincourt, Isabeau's last 'disgrace' was to agree to the Treaty of Troyes, although in fairness she had little choice about it, which dispossessed her son (later Charles VII) in favour of the heirs of Henry V of England and his new wife, Catherine (her own daughter).

Who preferred adultery to a pint of beer?

Nancy, Lady Astor, was the first woman to actually take up her seat in parliament and she quickly became known for her outspoken views, particularly on the subject of alcohol, which she was very much against. Opposing her on this crusade was the majority of the British male establishment, naturally enough, led by none other than Winston Churchill, who famously liked a drink, preferably champagne, at any time of day. Lady Astor, an American by birth, was not easily overawed by the looming form of a slightly inebriated establishment, however, and her quick wit could put even Churchill in his place. Perhaps her most famous put-down to the great man came after she invited him to a costume ball and he asked her what sort of disguise she would recommend for him. She replied: 'Why don't you come sober, Prime Minister?' Churchill got his own back with an even more famous exchange, when Lady Astor told him, 'If you were my husband I'd put arsenic in your coffee,' to which he replied, 'Madam, if I were your husband I'd drink it.'

The last laugh on the subject of temperance must go to the outspoken Labour MP Jack Jones, the man who had single-handedly ended the House of Commons tradition of quoting in Latin by shouting, 'And that is the winner of the two-thirty' at the top of his voice every time someone attempted it. When Lady Astor buttonholed him on the subject of the demon drink, she declared to him, 'I would rather commit adultery than drink a pint of beer.' Jones thought for a moment and then replied, 'Who wouldn't?'

Who said 'cock-a-doodle-doo' to a bishop?

Charles Beresford was something of a Victorian action man, maintaining parallel careers in the navy and the Houses of Parliament, which saw him fighting in Egypt and Sudan when not speaking in the Commons in favour of expanding the navy. He was also a great self-publicist, known to the newspapers as Charlie B, the embodiment of the John Bull spirit (in fact, he used to travel everywhere with his bulldog to reinforce this image). Popular both with the ladies and in royal circles, he became aide-de-camp to the Prince of Wales (later Edward VII) and in this capacity met the Countess of Warwick, Frances Evelyn Greville, known as Daisy to her friends. Daisy was the Prince of Wales's mistress at the time but she seems to have fallen genuinely in love with Beresford. The difficulty was that she was not discreet. Indeed, as the wife of Lord Brooke, she was known as 'the babbling Brooke' and provided the inspiration for the song 'Daisy, Daisy'. Her feelings for Beresford soon became well known to the prince, straining relations between the future king and his aide for the rest of their lives.

However, when it comes to indiscretion, it was Charles Beresford who must take the prize. At a house party shortly after their affair began, Beresford crept late one night into what he thought was Daisy's bedroom and leapt on to the bed with a cry of 'cock-a-doodle-doo!' After some frantic scrabbling around, a lamp was lit and Beresford found himself lying between the bishop of Chester and his wife, having broken into the wrong room. After this, it proved hard to keep the affair secret.

Who is the only member of the royal family to be sued for adultery?

Prince Henry Frederick, Duke of Cumberland (1745–90), the fourth son of Frederick Prince of Wales, was intended for a steady and none-too-public life in the navy. To this end he enrolled as a midshipman in 1768 and, as is sometimes the way with princes, had managed to make it to rear admiral just a year later.

Henry's real interests were very much on land, however, beginning and ending in the person of Harriet, Lady Grosvenor, wife of the 1st Baron Grosvenor. Their relationship began in the spring of 1769 and their habit of being seen openly together soon caused a minor scandal as well as infuriating her husband. Events reached a head around 2 a.m. on the morning of 22 December 1769 when Grosvenor's servants burst into a room at the White Hart Inn in St Albans and found Henry and Lady Grosvenor in bed together. Usually a prince might expect to walk away from such a scene in return for a favour or two granted to the husband or his family, but Grosvenor was incensed and chose to pursue Henry in the courts. On 5 July 1770 the prince was tried for 'criminal conversation' with Lady Grosvenor and found guilty, having to pay his lover's husband £10,000 in compensation – money he didn't have and which he had to borrow from his brother the king. The public took badly to what they saw as the state coffers paying out adultery fines for the royal family and the duke was pilloried in the press. Even the private correspondence of the two lovers managed to find its way into popular pamphlets where Henry was further ridiculed for his appalling English grammar.

Did George I go to bed with an elephant?

The arrival of the House of Hanover at the accession of George I brought to England a fascinating selection of foreign court creatures for the British aristocracy to observe, and none was more fascinating than Sophia Charlotte von Kielmansegg, Countess of Darlington. She was nominally the daughter of the Baron von Platen and his wife but was actually the illegitimate daughter of Duke Ernst August of Brunswick and Lüneburg and hence George I's half-sister. When he became king of Great Britain she followed him to England with her husband, who was made Master of Horse and started life as a courtier. She certainly made an impression on the English court. The young Horace Walpole described meeting her thus:

> Lady Darlington, whom I saw at my mother's in my infancy, and whom I remember by being terrified at her enormous figure, was as corpulent and ample as the duchess was long and emaciated. Two fierce black eyes, large and rolling beneath two lofty arched eyebrows, two acres of cheeks spread with crimson, an ocean of neck that overflowed and was not distinguished from the lower parts of her body, and no part restrained by stays – no wonder that a child dreaded such an ogress, and that the mob of London were highly diverted at the importation of so uncommon a seraglio!

From the above description it's perhaps not surprising that the London crowd soon had a nickname for the countess – the Elephant – as well as a rumour to attach to her. Her closeness to George I, and her insistence on openly competing with his mistresses (particularly the very thin Melusine von der Schulenburg, known as 'the Maypole') for his attention, led to the belief that she was having an affair with the king, even though she was his half-sister. In many minds this was perhaps just how the exotic German court behaved. The king's confectioner even went so far as to make public 'indecent suggestions' about the two, for which he promptly received his cards. Certainly Walpole believed that they had been lovers although this was probably more to do with the failure of the British aristocracy to understand how the Hanoverian court worked, and who had influence and why, than any proof he might have been privy to. The king's mother had written in 1701 to confide her 'certain knowledge' that the two were not having an affair and there is no conclusive evidence that at any later date George ever slept with his Elephant.

8

Ouch!

It is almost a definition of a gentleman to say that he is one who never inflicts pain.

John Henry Newman, *The Idea of a University* (1852)

What was the 'extraordinary question'?

The extraordinary question in question was actually a euphemism for a form of water torture, also known as the 'water cure'. The idea was to induce in the victim the sense that they were drowning. This was done quite simply by putting a clip on the victim's nose, a funnel or tube in their mouth and then pouring gallons of water (or sometimes urine) down their throat. In order not to suffocate, the subject would have to swallow the enormous quantity of liquid, leading to water intoxification and stomach cramps. When the prisoner was 'full' or unconscious, they would be beaten until they were sick and then the process was repeated.

The 'cure' was popular in seventeenth- and eighteenth-century France where it came in two varieties, the 'ordinary question', which consisted of just eight pints of water, and the 'extraordinary question', which consisted of sixteen pints. It was also used by the USA in the Philippines–American War of 1899–1902.

Which king died from a splinter?

Henry II of France did not come from a lucky family. He and his elder brother had spent three years of their childhood together in a Spanish cell after their art-loving father Francis I lost the Battle of Pavia to the Spanish and offered his boys as hostages in return for his own release. Later, Henry had only just become heir to the throne when his brother suddenly died after drinking a cup of water following a tennis match, something which, even then, was considered a little suspicious.

Henry's downfall came not via the machinations of his enemies, however, but during a celebration of his diplomatic skills. After the signing of the Treaty of Cateau-Cambrésis, between France, Spain and England in 1559, and celebrating the marriage of his daughter to the king of Spain, he decided to partake of a congratulatory joust, a favourite hobby of his, at the Place des Vosges in Paris. His opponent was one of his Scottish guards, Gabriel, Comte de Montgoméry, Seigneur de Lorges. The two men rode rapidly towards each other and clashed lances. The Comte de Montgoméry's lance shattered on impact, which was not particularly unusual in itself. It was only when the king reached the end of the tilting yard and turned back that the crowd realised something was very wrong. The heralds rushed to Henry's aid. The king had been wearing the protective armour usual for jousting, which covered the whole body and head, so he should have been well protected, were it not for a freak accident. What the heralds found was that a splinter of wood from the lance, two feet long, had somehow managed to shoot through the small slit in the visor of Henry's helmet, piercing his eye and brain, and exiting through his ear.

It took nine days for Henry to die from this terrible brain injury, during which his jealous wife, Catherine de Medici, deprived him of the company of his long-term mistress, Diane de Poitiers. The unfortunate de Montgoméry was pardoned of any wrong by Henry on his deathbed but still found himself in disgrace after the king's death. He later converted to Protestantism, the religion that Henry had spent his life trying to suppress, and he was one of the few to escape the St Bartholomew's Day massacre of Protestants orchestrated by Catherine de Medici. On his return to France from exile in England he was captured and beheaded.

How do you play mediaeval football?

The most characteristic English outdoor game of the mediaeval and Tudor periods, especially favoured by the working classes, was football. Mediaeval football was traditionally violent, loud, and dangerous – to bystanders as well as to players. The puritanical writer Philip Stubbes, who took against just about every form of recreation and pastime in his 1583 rant, 'The Anatomie of Abuses', describes the game thus: *'Football playing . . . may rather be called a friendly kind of fight, than a play, or recreation; A bloody and murdering practice, than a fellowly sport or pastime.'*

Football was a general term for a game involving a ball (usually a farm animal's bladder), two teams of indeterminate size and two 'goals', which could be several miles apart. Soccer (association football) is a nineteenth-century attempt to codify these games. Most football games in the sixteenth century would have involved two villages in what amounted to a running battle in which the ball was kicked, carried, hidden – whatever – between agreed 'goals', which might be village churches, trees, anything at all. There were not usually rules governing how you got the ball, so punching, kicking, tripping and gouging were all fine (although stabbing was frowned upon). Teams could consist of simply whoever turned up – whether ten people or a hundred – and players would come and go as the game might last for hours or even days. By 1600, with the introduction of the Reformation of Manners, these games were progressively proscribed as they encouraged drunkenness and riots, and were often associated with the old (and now prohibited) Catholic festivals. However, that didn't mean that people stopped playing them altogether. The most violent versions of football were known as 'camp-ball' in England, 'hurling' in Cornwall, or *cnapan* in Wales. In these games, a ball or other object was conveyed over open country to opposing goals by any means possible – even horsemen might be involved. These games frequently led to serious injuries and death.

Football was exclusively a male sport, but there were games with some violent content that might be played by both sexes. These might seem a little ludicrous but try them before you condemn them. In Hot Cockles, one player hid his head in another's lap while the others slapped him on the rear. If he could guess who had slapped him last, the two traded places. Blindman's Buff, also known as Hoodman Blind, was a similar game in which a blindfolded player tried to catch the others while they dealt him 'buffs' (blows). If he could identify the person he caught, they would trade places. In both of these games, men and women might play together, although they were more commonly played by boys and girls.

Similar to football in concept, if not equipment, was the game of bandy-ball, the ancestor of modern field hockey. The object of the game was to drive a small, hard ball through the opponents' goal with hooked clubs (almost identical to field hockey sticks).

Stoolball (which is still played in Hampshire to this day) was an ancestor of cricket and baseball, in which a stool was set on its side and players tried to hit the seat with a ball. In this game, women were expected to hike up their long skirts and play with the men. In the game of trap or trapball, the ball was placed on a device for casting it up in the air to be hit with a stick.

What did the Empress Irene, Ivan the Terrible, Süleyman the Magnificent and Constantine the Great have in common?

They all endangered their own family line by killing or attempting to kill their own eldest sons.

The Byzantine Empress Irene, who usually styled herself 'Emperor', such was her control over the empire, rubbed along perfectly happily with her son whilst he was a child but when he attempted to seize the throne for himself in AD 797 she captured him and had his eyes gouged out. Some sources say he died of his wounds shortly after, others that he survived his mother by a few years but in a terribly mutilated state. Either way, the family quickly fell from power.

Ivan the Terrible killed his son in 1581 after a family tiff. Ivan had beaten his son's wife for wearing immodest clothing, causing her to miscarry. Infuriated, the son had got into a heated argument with his father over this. At some point the argument got out of hand and Ivan struck his son on the head with his iron staff, killing him, albeit accidentally. On Ivan's death the Russian throne was inherited by his other son, Feodor I, known as Feodor the Bellringer, who was very devout but weak and probably mentally retarded. As he had no heir, Ivan's family line died out.

Süleyman the Magnificent's heir, Mustafa, had the disadvantage of not being the son of his favourite wife, Hurrem Sultan. As it was the custom on the succession of a new sultan for him to have his brothers strangled, Hurrem went about protecting her sons by starting a whispering campaign against Mustafa. Despite Mustafa's being easily the most talented and widely respected of Süleyman's sons, Süleyman came to believe the worst of him thanks to his wife's propaganda. Having been accused of treachery, Mustafa was invited by the sultan into his tent to defend himself. When he entered the tent, he was seized and murdered. Süleyman was then succeeded by one of Hurrem's sons, Selim, known as Selim the Sot, under whom the empire began to decay.

Constantine the Great's eldest son, Crispus, also fell prey to court machinations. His stepmother Fausta feared that Crispus would inherit the empire before her own three sons by Constantine and so she told the emperor that his son had propositioned her and then tried to rape her. On the basis of this, Constantine had his eldest son tried and executed in AD 326. Some months later he seems to have learnt that the incestuous affair was an invention of his wife's and he ordered her executed, too. According to one source, this was done by drowning her in a scalding-hot bath.

9

Magic

For I have sworn thee fair and thought thee bright,
who art as black as hell, as dark as night.

William Shakespeare, Sonnet 147

Why did Dick Whittington need a magical cat?

The extraordinary rise to prominence of Dick Whittington at a time
when the idea of social or financial improvement was entirely novel
has led to his becoming perhaps the only hard-nosed businessman
ever to make the transition to well-loved pantomime character. The
tale of Dick Whittington is one of the great success stories of a new
era of social mobility that grew out of the devastation of the Black
Death and so remarkable was his particular case that it was given
magical elements to help it.

Richard Whittington was not from the poorest class; indeed, his
father was a Gloucestershire knight, but as the third son he had little
chance of inheriting much land on his father's estate. Without land
(plus the social status and money that it brought) the only other
option open to Richard was to go to town and 'make his fortune'.
Before the Black Death the idea of simply moving away may have
seemed dangerous, if not impossible, to many in the country, but
with the aid of the City guilds Richard would do just that and
become an enormous success. Apprenticed in London, he went on
to become one of the leading lights of the Mercers' Guild, which
represented the cloth dealers. Cornering the extremely lucrative silk
and velvet market, he rapidly rose to prominence, selling to the
aristocracy, who thanks to the sumptuary laws were, at least in
theory, the only people who could wear his goods. He went on to
deal with the king himself, first selling Richard II two gold cloths
for £11 in 1389 in his first taste of what went on to become a hugely
profitable trade. When Richard II was deposed ten years later he
owed Whittington £1,000, which the mercer immediately recouped
by continuing the trade with the king's successor, Henry IV.

As he was three times master of the Guild and four times Mayor
of London, the trade in luxury cloth and wool made him one of the
richest merchants of his day. So great was his wealth in fact that it

became necessary to invent a reason for his success in a world where aspiration was a wholly new concept – hence the birth of the legend of his magical cat. To a mediaeval mindset – in which everyone was born into a station in life and died in that same station, where everybody had their set place – magic still seemed the only possible way that Dick Whittington could have been so successful. So Dick didn't need a magical cat, but those hearing of his perfectly genuine rise to fame and fortune needed him to have one.

Richard Whittington was grateful for the support that the Mercers' Guild had given him and, on his death, he pointedly left his huge estate (he died without heirs) not to the Church as his ancestors might have done, but to the Guild. At the time that estate was valued at £5,000, well in excess of £5 million in today's terms. The Mercers in return kept the name of Whittington alive, building almshouses, endowing the first Guildhall Library in London, funding a college of priests, making numerous bequests for church and hospital building, funding the rebuilding of Newgate gaol, and even commissioning a public lavatory. Even today the Mercers' Guild still runs the almshouses that bear Whittington's name.

Who was rescued by the Queen of Elfland?

The life of James IV of Scotland is quite well documented. It's what happened after his death that is something of a mystery.

Elves only ever pop up in historical narratives at times when no one is really all that certain what's going on and this was the case with James IV of Scotland. James was killed by the English at the disastrous Battle of Flodden Field, having invaded England in support of his French allies whilst Henry VIII was away on the continent.

Flodden was a massacre and after the battle it proved difficult to identify which body was James's. Eventually a likely candidate was found but this presented a new problem. James had died whilst under sentence of excommunication, having broken the Treaty of Eternal Peace with England. This had been brokered by the Borgia pope, Alexander VI, who agreed to excommunicate anyone who violated its terms.

James's body, therefore, could not be given Christian burial rites so it was taken to Berwick and embalmed, then sealed in lead and sent to Richmond Palace while everyone decided what to do with it. On his return from France, Henry VIII suggested that the body be buried in St Paul's but the pope refused to countenance this, so it was moved to the monastery at Sheen in Surrey and left there. In 1538 the problematic issue of the body resurfaced when the monastery was dissolved. James's remains were taken off show and put in an old lumber room. And that was the last place that James IV was ever seen.

There are three stories as to what happened next. One states that the body remained in the lumber room until the early years of the reign of Elizabeth I, at which time a glazier working in the partly demolished building reported the smell of embalming spices. A delegation duly arrived and inspected the remains but no further action was taken. Feeling now at liberty to do as he wished, the glazier then severed the head and took it home to show the family. Clearly they weren't too impressed so he took the head to the church of St Michael's, Wood Street, in the City of London, where he had it coffined and buried.

Whilst there is still a tradition that James's head is in St Michael's, according to the second story his body (with or without the head) rests in an unmarked grave in the grounds of Sheen monastery, although there is no documentary evidence for this.

Bearing that in mind, the third option, favoured in Scotland at the time of Flodden, is perhaps no less dubious. This states that James IV wasn't killed at all but was rescued by the Queen of Elfland and is even now waiting patiently for the day of his triumphant return.

10

Unsound Minds

As an experience, madness is terrific . . .

Virginia Woolf, letter to Ethel Smyth, 22 June 1930

What do French lawyers and rats have in common?

Bartholomew Chassenée was a famous sixteenth-century French jurist and, rather surprisingly, the rats were his clients. Prosecutions of animals were not as rare as you might reasonably expect in mediaeval and post-mediaeval Europe. The rats in Chassenée's case had been put on trial in the ecclesiastical courts for having 'feloniously eaten up and wantonly destroyed' a crop of barley. Set against the might of the French judicial system, you might imagine that the rats would have come off worst (let's face it, they did in Russia), particularly as they didn't show up for their trial. But never let it be said that such trials were unfair. The brilliant Chassenée, who was appointed as their counsel, argued that his clients probably didn't receive their summons since they had no fixed abode but moved from village to village. And even if they had received it and managed to read it, they were almost certainly far too frightened to come to the court in the town as that was where the cats lived. As cats ate rats, that meant that appearing in court put them in mortal danger – and that meant they could refuse the summons under French law. Chassenée went on to say that if the townsfolk could guarantee to keep their cats indoors and hence guarantee the safety of his clients, then they would answer the summons. As they were unable to do this, the judge dropped the case and the rats went free.

This was not an isolated case, however. In E. P. Evans's 1906 book, *The Criminal Prosecution and Capital Punishment of Animals*, he lists numerous legal cases brought against a range of animals. In 1494 a pig that clearly couldn't secure as good an attorney as Chassenée was tried and hanged near Clermont for having 'strangled and defaced a child in its cradle'. In 1519 some mice in Stelvio in the western Tyrol were convicted of damaging crops and ordered to leave – with the exception of expectant mothers and babies, who could not reasonably be made to leave in their current condition and were allowed to stay until they were fit enough to move on. A case against some flies in fourteenth-century Mayence rather backfired when their counsel managed to secure them a piece of land on which to retire. A group of lucky weevils at St Julien pulled off the same trick in 1587 when they were granted an estate some distance from the town in return for promising not to attack the local vineyards. In fact so confident were the weevils that they (or rather their human counsel) rejected the initial land offered as it wasn't good enough for them and secured a better plot instead. Less lucky animals included a sparrow accused of chattering in church and a cockerel convicted of laying an egg.

And before you put this down to some continental madness, in Britain a case was brought in AD 946 against a wooden statue that fell on a woman, killing her, and let's not forget the infamous 1535 Nottingham haystack trial.

Who liked kissing her dead husband's feet?

History has not been kind to Joanna of Castile. Despite being queen of Castile and mother to two Holy Roman Emperors, two queens of Portugal, a queen of France, a queen of Hungary and a queen of Denmark, she is known today simply as 'Joanna the Mad'.

The cause of Joanna's madness is disputed, not least by those who claim she wasn't mad at all but simply a pawn in a male game of power politics. However, she certainly displayed some unusual behaviour and the events of her life were, frankly, enough to drive anyone mad. Joanna was the daughter of Ferdinand and Isabella, the first joint rulers of a united Spain. In 1496 she was married to the dashing son of the Holy Roman Emperor, a lad whom history has more kindly granted the title 'Philip the Handsome'. It appears that he lived up to his name and Joanna fell deeply in love with him, to the point of obsession, beating her hands against the walls of her room when he refused to share a bed with her and attacking with scissors women at court whom she considered rivals for his affections. To be fair to her, her jealousy was not entirely misplaced. Philip was somewhat less than faithful and to avoid his wife's tantrums kept her a virtual prisoner.

If it was not a particularly happy life for the emotionally unstable Joanna, it was about to get much worse. In 1502, after the death of her brother, sister and her sister's child she became the heir to the throne of Spain. The powerbrokers of Europe therefore began to take a renewed interest in her – even her husband, who was hoping for a job as king of Spain. Sadly for him, and tragically for Joanna, Philip died in 1506, apparently of typhus, whilst only twenty-eight years old. Joanna took the death of her philandering, power-obsessed husband very badly and this seems to have hastened her mental decline. On the slow journey through Spain to his final resting place in Granada, she took to opening the coffin and caressing his body. In the first few days after his death no one really thought this unusual but after several months the regular opening of the coffin so that she could kiss his feet became a bit of a pungent ordeal – for everyone except Joanna.

With Joanna in such a vulnerable condition, her father Ferdinand took the opportunity to exploit her weakness and have himself declared co-regent of Castile (the title that his late wife had held). Meanwhile Joanna was becoming increasingly protective of her dead husband's body, refusing to allow it to rest in nunneries or be approached by women in case they became aroused by his rapidly decaying corpse. It was reported at the time that she had heard what sounds like a precursor to the story of Sleeping Beauty or Snow White – a legend of a fair prince who came back to life fourteen years after his apparent death – and so she resolved to wait by his coffin. However, she was not living in a fairy tale (although there's a fair chance that, like Snow White, Philip had been poisoned) and he remained resolutely dead.

Depending on whose side of the story you want to believe, her father either realised that Joanna was too ill to rule or he seized the opportunity to persuade the world that she was mad so that he could take control. Either way, he sent Joanna to the castle of Tordesillas where she was effectively imprisoned, the isolation only increasing her mental instability. Here she remained, until a revolt briefly freed her, but she failed to take advantage of her liberty. Her son, now king, suppressed the rebellion and had his mother locked in a single windowless room in the castle where she was held until her death some thirty-five years later. If she hadn't been mad when she married Philip, by the end of this life of cruel persecution she certainly was. Before she died it was said that she had become so terrified of people that she would run up the curtains of her cell like a cat when someone approached.

What did Alexandra of Bavaria believe she had swallowed?

Even the most staunch royalist would probably concede that the nineteenth-century Bavarian royal family had occasional mental health issues. Most famously the reclusive and paranoid Ludwig II had insisted on building fairy-tale castles that had nearly bank-rupted the state and led to his own deposition, but a history of madness ran deeper within the family. Ludwig's father, Maximilian II, was one of nine children who were all destined for the great royal houses of Europe. He would rule Bavaria, his little brother Otto would go on to become king of Greece, whilst their sisters Mathilde, Adelgunde and Hildegarde would marry a grand duke, a duke and an archduke respectively.

Then there was Alexandra Amalie, who was born in Aschaffenburg in 1826 in the Pompejanum – a peculiar replica of the house of Castor and Pollux at Pompeii. Her father had commissioned it as a country retreat and it was perhaps an early intimation of the family's unusual architectural preferences. She was the eighth of the nine children but whilst her brothers and sisters were tentatively stepping on to the world stage, Alexandra was not. Despite her slim figure and good looks (if we believe her portrait at least), her father did not want to bring Alexandra out in public. Initially this was due to the fact that she refused to wear any colour other than white. This is not of course in itself unique nor necessarily mad, but when the princess also began walking awkwardly, as though she was having difficulty negotiating around objects, it was considered wise to make an investigation. In the process Alexandra revealed that she had suffered an accident as a young child that had so upset her that she had kept it secret. The reason for her strange gait, she told her doctors, was that she had swallowed a grand piano (although one source claims that it was actually a glass sofa – not that that makes any more sense really). The inconvenience of walking around with such a large piece of furniture inside her was hence the explanation for her peculiar movements. Perhaps not surprisingly, Alexandra went on to become the only one of her brothers and sisters who reached adulthood not to marry. She died, aged forty-eight, in Munich on 8 May 1875.

11

Bang!

There is no terror in a bang, only in the anticipation of it.

Alfred Hitchcock, quoted in *Halliwell's Filmgoer's Companion* (1984)

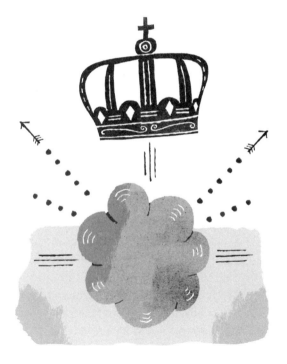

How long did the gunfight at the OK Corral last?

Despite being immortalised in novels and movies, the gunfight at the OK Corral on the afternoon of Wednesday, 26 October 1881, lasted only about thirty seconds. During that time, between twenty and thirty shots were fired from a range of about ten feet. At the end of it, however, Billy Clanton and Frank and Tom McLaury were left dead or dying. Three members of the Clanton gang survived unscathed by very wisely running away when the shooting started: Billy's brother Ike, who was probably unarmed; Billy Claiborne (again probably unarmed); and Wes Fuller. On the other side, Wyatt Earp emerged unscathed, Doc Holliday received a graze to the hip, whilst Virgil Earp and Morgan Earp received wounds in the calf and back respectively.

Billy Clanton and the McLaurys were buried at the Boot Hill Cemetery in Tombstone. There are at least eighteen Boot Hill cemeteries in the US, the name being given to burial grounds for those who 'died with their boots on' or, in other words, died a violent death. These cemeteries were also used for paupers' graves.

How could Annie Oakley have prevented the First World War?

Phoebe Ann Mosey was born in 1860 into a poor family in Ohio, and from the age of nine learnt to shoot game to provide an income for her mother and siblings. So good in fact did Phoebe become at shooting that she began taking part in local competitions with sharpshooters, and it was through one of these that she met her future husband and began her famous career. Starting out as her husband's assistant, she soon outshone him and he became her manager instead. By the time the two of them joined Buffalo Bill's Wild West Show in 1885, she had taken the professional name Annie Oakley and her name was known across the USA. In 1887 the show toured Europe and attracted royal patronage, including a performance given for Queen Victoria. It also was on this tour that Annie briefly, and unknowingly, got her chance to change history.

Crown Prince Wilhelm, very shortly to become Kaiser Wilhelm II, had heard of her famous trick in which she shot the ash off the end of a cigarette held in her husband's teeth. He insisted that she perform the trick on him but, perhaps unwilling to take too great a risk, she persuaded him to hold the cigarette in his hand rather than between his lips. She then became perhaps the only person ever to point a loaded firearm at Wilhelm. It is a tragedy for world history that she proved that, even under these stressful conditions, she was an excellent shot. She hit the ash on the cigarette, leaving the Shakespeare-loving Kaiser unscathed – something she is later claimed to have quite regretted.

Who ruined the Parthenon?

The Parthenon had stood on the Acropolis of Athens since the fifth century BC and survived being converted into a Christian church in the sixth century AD as well as a mosque following the Turkish capture of Athens in 1458. Whilst both Christians and Muslims had made some alterations to the building, it remained remarkably intact until 1687. In that year the Venetians, under Francesco Morosini, attacked Athens and the defending Ottomans fortified the Acropolis, turning the Parthenon into a gunpowder magazine. The result was predictable. On 26 September a Venetian mortar battery, set up on the Hill of Philopapus, opened fire on the Acropolis. One mortar achieved a direct hit on the powder magazine in the Parthenon and the building exploded. All the internal structures were destroyed, the tops were ripped from many of the pillars on the south side and the roof collapsed. In the process, many of the famous sculptures on the building were hurled to the ground and broken. Shortly after this act of vandalism, Morosini did capture the city and returned to Venice loaded with plaudits (as well as bits of the Parthenon). In 1688 he was elected doge.

Which English king exploded?

According to the chronicler Ordericus Vitalis, William the Conqueror had a very unseemly end. He had fallen sick at Rouen after receiving abdominal injuries from his saddle pommel when he fell off his horse at the siege of Mantes, and was taken to a small lodge just outside the city. There, his condition rapidly worsened and he became racked with stomach pains. Realising that his time had come, he summoned his sons and nobles and made preparation for what he knew would be a messy succession.

According to Vitalis, William didn't hold out much hope for his soul either, telling them:

> I tremble, my friends, when I reflect on the grievous sins which burden my conscience, and now, about to be summoned before the awful tribunal of God, I know not what I ought to do. I was bred to arms from my childhood, and am stained from the rivers of blood I have shed. It is out of my power to count all the injuries which I have caused during the sixty-four [he was actually probably fifty-nine] years of my troubled life.

He did, however – at least according to the rather pro-William chroniclers who recorded the event – make lengthy confessions, divide up his lands and extensive treasure, and decide what should be done with some of his more troublesome prisoners, before finally expiring on 9 September 1087.

It was now that events started to get a little unseemly. The nobles who had been with the king immediately fled back to their own estates to secure them against any possible conflict over the succession, leaving the king's body in the charge of their retainers. Depending on how you look at it, these individuals now either quite sensibly took the opportunity to improve their pension prospects in what had suddenly become a considerably more uncertain world, or behaved rather badly. According to Vitalis, *'the inferior servants, observing that their masters had disappeared, laid hands on the arms, the plate, the robes, the linen, and all the royal furniture, and leaving the corpse almost naked on the floor of the house, they hastened away.'*

Eventually a local knight brought the dead king's rapidly putrefying and swollen body to St Stephen's church in Caen for burial. However, there were to be further delays. During the funeral procession a fire broke out in the town and most of the mourners left to put it out. When the service finally began it was immediately interrupted by a local man called Ascelin who loudly announced that he owned the land on which William was to be buried but had never been paid for it. Eventually he was given sixty shillings and the service continued. The remaining monks who were not putting out fires or paying off irate landowners then tried to squeeze William's now very bloated corpse into a stone sarcophagus but, as Vitalis says, *'they were obliged to use some violence in forcing [the body] in, . . . so that, as the king was very corpulent, the bowels burst, and an intolerable stench affected the bystanders . . . The priests therefore hurried the conclusion of the funeral service and retired as soon as possible, in great alarm, to their respective abodes.'*

William's body was finally interred at Caen and remained there until 1562 when his tomb was completely destroyed by Calvinists. Only his left thigh bone was saved from destruction, which was later reinterred in a new tomb. This too fell prey to rioters during the

French revolution in 1793 and now only a stone slab marks where William the Conqueror once lay.

What nineteenth-century game involved smashing snail shells?

The name 'conker' comes from the nineteenth-century dialectal word *conker* meaning snail shell, as the game was originally played using garden snail shells. A regional variant used hazelnuts. The first recorded game of conkers using horse chestnuts was on the Isle of Wight in 1848. Conkers are also known regionally as 'obblyonkers' or 'cheggies'. The World Conker Championships began by accident in Ashton in 1965 when a group of regulars at the local pub were prevented from going fishing by bad weather. They decided to play conkers instead, giving the entrance fees to charity and instituting a small prize for the winner.

12

Unlucky

Some folk want their luck buttered.

Thomas Hardy, *The Mayor of Casterbridge* (1886), chapter 13

What was the Ball of the Burning Men?

This unfortunate incident was definitely not the sort of party you'd want to get invited to.

In the first week of 1393 the French court decided to celebrate the forthcoming third marriage of one of the queen's ladies-in-waiting with a party. As part of the festivities, the king, Charles VI, known rather worryingly to history as Charles the Mad, decided that he and a few friends would dress up as wild men, chain themselves together and dance around. Keen to look the part, the king ordered costumes made of linen soaked in pitch on to which were stuck strands of frayed hemp, making them look appropriately hairy and wild. It was also pointed out that they bore a striking resemblance to unlit candles and so all naked flames were banned from the event.

It seems, however, that no one had mentioned this to the king's brother, Louis, Duc d'Orléans, who appeared during the revels at the Hôtel St Pol with a lighted torch. Sadly the inevitable happened. One of the dancing wild men strayed too close to the torch and promptly burst into flames. As he careered around trying to put himself out, he soon set light to other dancers and pandemonium ensued. At this point the heroic Duchesse de Berri, who was only fourteen at the time, came to the fore. She recognised King Charles and hid him under her skirts, thus protecting him from the flames. The others were not so lucky. The combination of pitch and hemp burnt furiously and whilst one dancer managed to save himself by jumping into a barrel of water, the Comte de Joigny burnt to death on the spot. Yvain de Foix and Aimery Poitiers died of their burns two days later and Huguet de Guisay, who was blamed for coming up with the whole silly idea, followed them to the grave the following day. The event went down in history as the Bal des Ardents – the 'Ball of the Burning Men'.

Who has the record for the shortest reign?

Dom Luis of Portugal's is perhaps one of the unhappier entries in the book of Royal records. Luis's father, King Carlos I, had come to the throne of Portugal in 1889 but his reign was marked by social unrest. His extramarital affairs and financial extravagance made him unpopular, particularly as the country twice went bankrupt under his reign, as did his appointment of an authoritarian government. On 1 February 1908 as the royal family were returning to the palace in Lisbon, shots were fired at their carriage as it passed through Terreiro do Paço Square. Carlos was hit and died instantly, leaving his heir Luis Felipé as king. Unfortunately he had been mortally wounded too and, after reigning, uncrowned, for just twenty minutes, he also died.

Even Luis Felipé's single claim to fame is disputed. Following the 'July Revolution' of 1830 in France, Charles X was forced to abdicate by a delegation of the people sent to the Tuileries. At the moment that he signed the abdication document, his heir, Louis Antoine, became King Louis XIX. Louis XIX, however, was not at all sure that he wanted to be king and an extraordinary scene ensued, in which the former King Charles sat crying in the corner whilst Louis XIX's wife desperately tried to persuade her husband to accept the throne. After twenty minutes Louis tired of this drama and abdicated as well.

Who gave his name to nationalistic zealotry?

Nicholas Chauvin is remembered today for the one word that he brought to the English language – chauvinism. Separating the real Chauvin from the mythical is no easy matter but he appears in fact to have been a rather brave soldier in the First Army of the French Republic and then latterly in Napoleon's Grande Armée. Having enlisted at eighteen, he fought fervently for the new France, being wounded seventeen times and becoming badly disfigured in the process. Indeed, so valiant was Chauvin that Napoleon himself awarded him a pension – along with a nice sword. After the fall of Napoleon, however, a wave of disenchantment swept over France. Men like Chauvin, who had shown such idealism and unswerving loyalty, were ridiculed and Chauvin himself was cruelly caricatured in plays as a blindly nationalistic fool. His largely invented exploits and opinions, as disseminated in these plays, led to the coining of the word chauvinism to describe unthinking nationalistic zeal.

Why might it be dangerous to drink weak beer?

Thomas Thetcher, according to his tombstone outside Winchester Cathedral, made the fatal mistake of drinking beer that wasn't strong enough on a hot day. All that we know about Thomas comes from his tombstone, which has been lovingly preserved and, where necessary, replaced by generations of Hampshire Grenadiers – the regiment to which Thomas belonged. The stone begins with the basic facts of the case:

> In memory of Thomas Thetcher
> a grenadier in the North regiment
> of Hants Militia, who died of a
> violent fever contracted by drinking
> small beer when hot on the 12th May 1764
> Aged 26 years . . .

Small beer was a common drink throughout the mediaeval period and well into the nineteenth century, as the boiling of the water used to make it and the presence of a low level of alcohol in it killed bacteria and generally made it much safer than water. Just how small beer killed Thomas is uncertain although a series of letters in 1999 to the distinguished *New England Journal of Medicine* suggested 'deglutition syncope', a condition where drinking cold liquids can lead to fainting.

Thomas's fellow soldiers were less interested in the exact cause and more in the lessons to be drawn from it. The tombstone goes on: *'In grateful remembrance of whose universal good will towards his Comrades, this Stone is placed here at their expense, as a small testimony of their regard and concern.'* Then it breaks into verse:

> Here sleeps in Peace a Hampshire Grenadier
> Who caught his death by drinking cold small beer
> Soldiers be wise from his untimely fall
> And when ye're hot drink strong or not at all.

Having turned the story of Thomas from a warning against drink to an exhortation to drink something stronger, the Hampshire Grenadiers have been keen to preserve their monument, adding other suitable lines as and when necessary. The gravestone continues with an affectionate rededication:

> THIS MEMORIAL BEING DECAY'D WAS RESTOR'D BY THE
> OFFICERS OF THE GARRISON A.D. 1781.
>
> AN HONEST SOLDIER NEVER IS FORGOT
> WHETHER HE DIE BY MUSKET OR BY POT.

Since then the North Hampshire Militia and the Royal Hampshire Regiment have both taken their turns in replacing the stone when it has decayed. Today an annual service is still held at the graveside.

What made William the Miserable so unhappy?

William was the son of Robert, Duke of Normandy, and grandson of the explosive William the Conqueror and should therefore have been a pretty powerful figure in twelfth-century European politics. Although he should have inherited the wealthy duchy of Normandy, this was sequestered by his uncle, Henry I, who captured and imprisoned Robert in 1106. Robert was kept in such great luxury that he rather took to it and made no attempt to escape, leaving his son to wander around Europe. William made several attempts to regain his duchy but they all failed and for twenty years he was homeless. Eventually he became engaged to the daughter of the Count of Anjou, which meant that he could look forward to a sizeable dowry and inheritance from the match, but the marriage was blocked at the last minute by dear old Uncle Henry.

Then, in 1128, the Count of Flanders died without an heir and William managed to persuade the French king to back his somewhat tenuous claim to the title. The French king gave William an army and he marched to Flanders. In the meantime, the nobles of Flanders had already chosen a new count, Thierry of Alsace. The two sides clashed at Thielt where, in a brilliant manoeuvre, William outflanked and defeated Thierry, which was about the only good piece of fortune in his entire life. William now ruled Flanders and soon heard that the nobles of Normandy had asked for him as their duke (rather than Matilda, Henry's daughter). William immediately made plans to take up the dukedom, but on his way came upon a small skirmishing party of Uncle Henry's troops. William received a cut in the fight, which turned septic, and he died in agony five days later.

13

How Did That Happen?

It happened one day, about noon . . .

Daniel Defoe, *Robinson Crusoe* (1719)

How did Erik Bloodaxe get his name?

Many early Scandinavian leaders took (or were given) epithets that said something about who they were, from the fairly obvious 'Gorm the Old' to the more puzzling 'Ivarr the Boneless'. Erik falls comfortably into the first category.

On the death of their father Harald Finehair, the first king of Norway, his sons quickly set about trying to consolidate their own positions by murdering each other. The first victim was Bjørn the Seaman, who was surrounded whilst having a drink at Tønsberg by Erik and his men. According to Harald Harfager's saga, Bjørn and his friends put up a good fight but in the end Erik killed him, which didn't make Erik too popular in that part of the country. Olaf, another (half) brother, then tried to make himself king of eastern Norway, supported by another (half) brother, Sigrød, which rather annoyed Erik. The three men met in battle just outside Tønsberg where Erik notched up another two dead brothers and gained the Latin title 'brother-slayer' or the rather more visual Viking title 'bloodaxe'. Unfortunately for Erik, his run of fratricidal luck was about to run out. In 933 the youngest brother, Haakon, returned from England and ousted Erik, who was forced to flee to Northumbria where he became king with his capital at Jorvik (York). He died in battle, as someone called Bloodaxe probably should, at Stainmoor in 954. Haakon meanwhile became king of all Norway and received the much nicer title, 'Haakon the Good'.

Why did Joan of Arc fight the English?

At the time of Joan of Arc's campaign, France was legally a possession of the descendants of Henry V of England, as laid out in the Treaty of Troyes, which had been signed by the French king, Charles VI, following the defeat of his army at Agincourt. In the treaty Charles had declared his son illegitimate (which was quite likely) and made the children of his son-in-law, Henry V, his heirs – so what did Joan have to complain about? The simple reason was that when Charles had signed the document, he was completely mad.

The first attack of the schizophrenia from which Charles would suffer for the rest of his life did not occur until 1392, during a campaign against the man who had attempted to assassinate one of his councillors. On 5 August, a very sultry summer's day, the king and his entourage were riding towards the Breton borders. Charles, who had drunk a great deal of wine, was wearing a thick velvet jacket and a velvet hat, which in itself was bizarre enough. His brother and uncles were with him but at a distance as the road was very dusty.

When the group reached the edge of the forest of Le Mans, a roughly dressed man stepped out from behind a tree and seized the bridle of the king's horse, shouting, 'Ride no further, noble king! Turn back! You are destroyed!' The king's attendants forced the man to release the bridle but strangely enough he was not arrested, perhaps because they simply assumed him to be deranged.

Later that day, as the cavalcade was emerging from the forest into the open plain, one of the king's pages, drowsy with the heat, dropped the king's lance, which fell on to his neighbour's steel helmet with a clatter. Charles was startled by the sound and drew his sword, shouting, 'Forward against the traitors! They wish to deliver me to the enemy!' He then struck out at all those around him, killing four or five of his own knights, including the Chevalier de Polignac. The Duke of Burgundy shouted, 'My God, the king is out of his mind! Hold him, someone!' Charles was eventually disarmed and taken down from his horse. He lay prostrate on the ground, speechless, his eyes rolling wildly from side to side. Eventually he was placed on an ox-cart and taken back to Le Mans.

This incident marked the beginning of a series of episodes of madness in which the king would variously forget who he and his family and friends were, and he spent his nights running through his palaces howling like a wolf. Towards the end of his life he also became delusional, believing that he was made of glass and might shatter if touched. As a result many in France, including Joan of Arc, believed that his signature on the Treaty of Troyes wasn't worth the paper it was written on and a campaign began to restore the French monarchy to a French ruler.

Why did Lady Godiva get her kit off?

Lady Godiva, or Godgifu to give her her Anglo-Saxon name, was a real historical character, although stories about her dress sense have been wildly exaggerated in later centuries. She was the wife of Earl Leofric of Mercia, a successful and by all accounts rather pious noble who managed to steer a political path through the reigns of Cnut, Harold Harefoot, Harthacnut and Edward the Confessor – something that would impress you if you'd met any of them. According to the legend, however, he was a harsh landlord who had inflicted heavy taxes upon the people of Coventry, much to the disgust of his wife. In the earliest version of the tale, recorded by Roger of Wendover around the late twelfth or early thirteenth centuries, Leofric, exasperated by Godiva's nagging, eventually agreed to lift the taxes if she would ride naked through the market in Coventry in front of all the citizens. He clearly thought that she would never do something so humiliating but she, with a flourish, let down her floor-length hair, which he obviously hadn't noticed she'd grown but which handily covered her modesty. She then mounted her horse and, accompanied by two knights, rode through Coventry in front of all and sundry, none of whom got a glimpse of anything more saucy than a bit of leg. Leofric therefore kept his word and waived the taxes. So it would be fair to say that Godiva rode through Coventry naked for tax reasons.

In still later versions of the story, Godiva protected her modesty by issuing a decree that everyone in Coventry should stay indoors whilst she rode through town so that no one would see her. By the seventeenth century this story had received a new wrinkle when one inhabitant, Thomas by name, is said to have decided to bore a hole in the shutters of his house so that he could glimpse the lovely Godiva as she rode past. Unfortunately for Thomas, as she rode into view he was struck blind, and at that moment the legend of 'Peeping Tom' was born.

None of this actually bears much relation to the real Godiva, though. Coventry was not subject to particularly harsh or arbitrary taxes more than anywhere else and the town was probably a personal possession of Godiva's rather than Leofric's (important Saxon women held land in their own right). Indeed, Godiva is one of only a handful of Anglo-Saxon landowners who managed to hold on to their property after the Norman conquest. Nor would it have been that impressive to ride through the city naked as Coventry was really more of a hamlet at the time. Indeed, in the Domesday survey of 1086, only sixty-nine families are recorded as living there, and amongst their houses there was nowhere suitable for Leofric and Godiva to have being staying whilst they had the famous argument anyway. In truth, Godiva and her husband were pious benefactors of the Church and no harsher landlords than any other. All early sources agree that Godiva was a generous and good woman and none mentions the naked ride, which you might think they would have done if it had happened. If there is a grain of truth in the Godiva story, it is perhaps that she, as the owner of Coventry, rode through the village as a penitent (i.e. in plain dress) as part of a benefaction to the monastery there.

How did Calamity Jane get her name?

Martha Jane Burke (née Canary) was better known in her day as Calamity Jane. Sorting out the biographical details of her life is tricky as she was rather prone to exaggeration in her own memoirs. We know that she was born in 1855 in Missouri and that both her parents had died by the time she was twelve. In 1870 she signed on as a US army scout (although it is unclear whether she actually enlisted in the army) and over the next six years she was involved in a number of campaigns in the Indian Wars. During this time she claimed that she was under Custer's command but this seems unlikely.

It was during this period that she got her nickname 'Calamity', although there are two versions of how this came about. She claims in her *Life and Adventures of Calamity Jane* that, during the splendidly named Nursey Pursey Indian Outbreak, her unit was ambushed and her commander, Captain Egan, shot. She turned to see him reeling in the saddle and, galloping back, caught him, swung him on to her horse and rode the two of them to the safety of the nearest fort. When Captain Egan recovered, he supposedly christened her Calamity, presumably for saving him from one. The alternative story, prevalent even during her lifetime, was that she got the name due to her repeated warnings that a calamity would befall anyone who crossed her.

In 1876, Calamity ended up in the gold-strike town of Deadwood, South Dakota, where she met Wild Bill Hickok whom she later claimed she had married and had borne a daughter. In truth Wild Bill was shot dead in a saloon not long after they met and was at the time newly and happily married, so this is fairly improbable. Being associated with Wild Bill never hurt the reputation of a frontierswoman, however, particularly one who was already becoming the focus of early magazine stories about 'how the West was won'. In 1891, Calamity did marry but not happily and five years later she began touring with the new 'Wild West' shows. Her erratic behaviour and alcoholism did not endear her to show managers and eventually she returned to Deadwood, where she died in poverty in 1903. Her last wish was granted and she was buried next to Wild Bill Hickok.

14

Who?

'Whom are you?' he asked, for he had attended business college.

George Ade, 'The Steel Box', in the *Chicago Record*, 16 March 1898

Why were there 212 fatalities at the first boy scout camp?

There wasn't much dybbing and dobbing at Robert Baden-Powell's first scout camp as the camp in question was in Mafeking and took place during a particularly nasty siege in the Second Boer War. Baden-Powell had been sent to Cape Colony to raise two new regiments to fight the Boers who at this point seemed to be winning their war against the British Empire. He was already a well-known figure thanks to the publication, in book form and in newspaper articles, of his role in the Ashanti and Zulu campaigns. He had also managed a stint in secret intelligence, collecting news from around the Mediterranean whilst disguised as a butterfly collector. But by the time he arrived in Cape Colony in 1899, now a lieutenant-colonel, he had still not made the impression he hoped for. Mafeking would change that.

Baden-Powell met considerable resistance in the Cape and, with the Boers closing in, eventually concluded that the best form of attack was defence. Taking and fortifying the strategically import-ant town of Mafeking, he held it against Boer besiegers with a force of about 2,000, including a unit of boys who served as messengers and orderlies. Outgunned and outnumbered, Baden-Powell was forced to use every trick and stratagem he knew, including ostentatiously laying a field of (fake) mines and getting his troops to act as though they were picking their way through (imaginary) barbed wire to keep the besiegers at bay.

After a siege lasting 217 days, and costing 212 lives amongst Baden-Powell's men, they were relieved by the arrival of a British force that included his own brother, Major Baden Fletcher Smyth Powell (who changed his name by royal licence in 1902 to the even more elaborate Baden Fletcher Smyth Baden-Powell).

As the Boer War had been going badly for the British, the news of Baden-Powell's plucky resistance at Mafeking, and its heroic relief, caused the British press to go wild. Baden-Powell was fêted as a hero and the verb to 'maffick' (to wildly celebrate) briefly entered the English language, at least in the minds of journalists. His famous exploits in keeping the Boers at bay also made his book, *Aids to Scouting for NCOs and Men*, an unexpected bestseller and, following a meeting with the founder of the Boys' Brigade, he agreed to rewrite this book for children. Although there is no evidence that the 'boy scouts' used at Mafeking were directly organised by Baden-Powell, he does seem to have been impressed by their resilience and he mentions them in the first chapter of *Scouting for Boys*. This, too, was a great success and as a result scout groups began spontaneously forming all over the country. Under the guidance of Baden-Powell and his wife, this grew into the international Scouting and Guiding movement which now has over thirty-eight million members.

Baden-Powell is buried near his last home in Kenya. His grave carries the trail sign of a circle with a dot in the middle, meaning, 'I have gone home.'

Which world leader drew the poster for Teddy's Perspiration Powder?

Quite a few world leaders have considered themselves to be great artists too, notably Nero, who toured the festivals of Greece, winning plaudits and laurels with only the help of his innate genius and a heavily armed bodyguard to intimidate the judges. Not all aspiring artists have had it quite so easy, however, particularly one young man hammering on the door of the Vienna Fine Art School in 1907. He took the entrance examination that year but, greatly to his own surprise, was rejected on the grounds that his test drawing was 'unsatisfactory'. He therefore tried again the following year but did not even make the grade to sit the examination. Thus it was that the brilliant career of one young man was smothered before it had even begun.

He spent another five years in Vienna, living hand-to-mouth (as many a great artist has done), although he did get through an inordinate number of cream cakes, and in that time produced by his own reckoning over a thousand watercolours. As few of these sold, he was reduced to painting advertising hoardings for local shopkeepers, including one for Teddy's Perspiration Powder, a jolly image of Santa selling coloured candles, and the magnificent spire of St Stephen's Cathedral rising out of a pile of soap cakes. Eventually he decided to cut his losses and leave the city of his artistic dreams. The First World War was looming and Adolf Hitler was going to enlist. A new career awaited.

Who was Dirty Dick?

The original Dirty Dick was an ironmonger called Nathaniel Bentley, known as 'The Beau of Leadenhall Street'. Life was not to be kind to Dick and when his bride-to-be died on the night before their wedding, he sealed up the room in which he had prepared their wedding banquet and became a recluse. Refusing to wash or change his clothes, he soon became a famous, if tragic, character in the City. After fifty years in business, Bentley finally retired in 1804 and moved away, when it was discovered that he had made his shop on Leadenhall Street into a shrine to lost love. The interior was as though half a century had not passed. Everything had been left where it was on that terrible evening. Even his cats lay where they had died, and inside the locked room the desiccated remains of the never-eaten wedding banquet still stood on the dust-covered table.

The English love an eccentric and by this time Dirty Dick was already a celebrity, inspiring the landlord of the Old Port Wine Shop in Bishopsgate to buy the contents of his ironmongers, lock, stock and barrel, carefully transporting it in its filthy state to his pub, which he renamed Dirty Dick's. This peculiar attraction remained on show in the City until the 1980s when the collection fell foul of health and safety regulations and had to be cleaned up. Dirty Dick's memory lives on, however, preserved in the pub's name and immortalised in Dickens' *Great Expectations*, in which he was the inspiration for Miss Havisham.

Which twentieth-century British king was murdered?

George V was not a man to mince his words, certainly not when he was feeling poorly. A famous story relates that, as he lay on his deathbed, some courtiers tried to cheer the dying king by suggesting that he would soon be well enough to visit Bognor Regis. Aware that he would never rise from his bed again, he caustically replied, 'Bugger Bognor!' and promptly expired.

Sadly this is probably untrue. The king's librarian, Sir Owen Morshead, told a different variant of the story. He claims that when the good burghers of Craigwell came to see the king to ask whether they might change its name to Bognor Regis, the king told his private secretary (who presented the petition), 'Bugger Bognor!' The ever-diplomatic Private Secretary translated this back to the citizens of Craigwell as, 'His Majesty would be graciously pleased to grant your request.'

Perhaps more interesting than George V's last words is the fact that he was murdered (well, technically speaking). On 15 January 1936, the king had retired to his bedroom at Sandringham, feeling ill. By 20 January he was comatose and clearly dying but still clinging to life, which presented his doctor, Lord Dawson, with a problem. He didn't want the king's family left in limbo for days. In Dawson's opinion, the world at large would be better served by hearing of the king's death in the morning papers rather than in what he sniffily referred to as 'the evening journals'. So he decided to kill him. Conveniently, the King was entirely insensible and felt nothing. Having written the famous bulletin, 'The life of the king is moving peacefully to its close,' on his menu card at dinner, he went upstairs to hurry it along a bit. His Sandringham diaries, first brought to light by Francis Watson in 1986, reveal how he did it: *'I therefore decided to determine the end and injected (myself) morphia gr.3/4 and shortly afterwards cocaine gr.1 into the distended jugular vein: 'myself' because it was obvious that Sister B [the king's nurse] was disturbed by the procedure.'*

This did the trick and the king died peacefully, surrounded by his family, at about five minutes to midnight, in good time to catch the headlines in the morning broadsheets. Later that year Dawson voted against a euthanasia bill passing through the House of Lords.